YOU CAN HAVE
GOD'S HELP WITH
DAILY PROBLEMS

YOU CAN HAVE
GOD'S HELP WITH
DAILY PROBLEMS

NORMAN VINCENT PEALE

SPECIAL FCL EDITION

FOUNDATION FOR CHRISTIAN LIVING
PAWLING, NEW YORK 12564

Printed in the United States of America
Library of Congress Catalog Card No. 79-57646

Introduction

WHAT PUBLICATION could have a more important purpose than to help the reader secure God's help in human problems?

We all have problems and all of us need help in meeting and handling them. Human help is important, but God's help is vital. In this book both are available.

You Can Have God's Help with Daily Problems is designed to help you in a practical and workable way. And the principles upon which it is based are spiritual in nature as well as practical in application. We truly believe that if the reader will read, study and apply the suggestions made here, he or she will achieve the wonderful result of having the guidance and help of God in human problems as never before experienced.

This book does a number of things. It tells of the wonderful promises of the Bible in Part One. Part Two talks about the value of enthusiasm; Part Three shows how you can overcome any problem. In the fourth Part is outlined what to do, what attitudes to have, what steps to take when you are confronted with a hard fact, a troublesome situation. Part Five contains suggestions about the power to change your life. Part Six outlines the type of thoughts that will build faith within you. And finally, in Part Seven, we provide the Pocket Cards which have helped hundreds of thousands to find God's ways in their problems.

These Parts of *You Can Have God's Help with Daily Problems* have previously been published individually by the Foundation for Christian Living and, judging by the vast mail response over the years, have been immensely helpful to many persons. They are available to the reader in individual booklet form (see below).

Therefore, on this, the 40th Anniversary of the Foundation for Christian Living, we deemed it an outstanding service to bring all of this material into one publication. By this means, all of our readers can have the booklets, which may have previously inspired them, in one place. And new readers can have the benefit of previously published material to help them in their human problems.

For 40 years the Foundation for Christian Living (FCL) has offered all of its publications on a voluntary contribution basis. Its publishing work is supported by gifts, large, medium and small. This organization which teaches faith, survives and provides services by faith in the belief that as readers are helped personally they will, in turn, help FCL to keep on assisting them and, in addition, to reach out to an ever-increasing number of people.

Any reader may request individual booklets by name, or any of the seven pocket cards, and receive a list of all our publications by writing to: FCL, Pawling, New York 12564.

Finally, you should know that we issue monthly a magazine type publication called "Creative Help for Daily Living" that goes into hundreds of thousands of homes on the same voluntary contribution basis. You are invited to become a regular recipient of this publication, which will bring spiritual and motivational inspiration to you regularly. Simply write to the above mentioned address.

On our 40th Anniversary we send you this book of inspiration with a sincere prayer that it may bring God's help to you in your human problems as you face them day by day.

Norman Vincent Peale

CONTENTS

PART ONE:
Wonderful Promises

PART TWO:
Enthusiasm!
The *Action* Handbook

PART THREE:
You Can Overcome Any Problem!

PART FOUR:
What to Do When

WHAT TO DO WHEN . . .

PART FIVE:
The Power to Change Your Life

THE SEVEN-POINT FORMULA:

PART SIX:
Faith Builders

PART SEVEN:
The Pocket Cards

YOU CAN HAVE
GOD'S HELP WITH
DAILY PROBLEMS

PART ONE:

Wonderful Promises

31 Promises that Can Change Your Life

HOW TO USE
Wonderful Promises
IN YOUR LIFE

This section contains some of the most wonderful promises ever made. And they are all for you. You can count on every one of them since they are taken word for word from the most reliable source in existence, the Holy Bible. They are God's promises. So read them, study them, believe them and live on them.

You will find here thirty-one carefully selected promises, one for each day in the month. I suggest that you first read these promises in their entirety so as to get a comprehensive feel of the spiritual wealth they present. You cannot help being inspired, even thrilled, by reading these thirty-one amazing promises of God.

Then, I hope you will work with one promise each day, reading both it and the explanatory paragraph. Spend a few minutes in meditation upon it and think of the promise in a highly personal way, relating it specifically to yourself. Say to yourself, "This promise is for me personally. I hereby accept it and make it my own. I will use it this day in all my problems."

To make it really your own you must go beyond this affirmation and insert the promise deeply into your mind, into your very consciousness. This may be accomplished first by committing it to memory. So, each day say the promise over and over, meanwhile picturing it as becoming indelibly printed upon your mind. This will fix it as a mental and spiritual possession. Then make it the last

3

thing you say before going to sleep at night.

The next day repeat this process with promise number two, meanwhile reviewing the first promise. If you perform this plan faithfully, on the last or thirty-first day you will be able to repeat from deep spiritual memory thirty-one great promises made to you and to all of us by God.

Each time you face a problem or a difficulty or a disappointment or any one of the many crises life brings, just start to surround that matter with all these promises of help, support and guidance. As you marshall the promises with all their power you will find that your problem, which seemed very strong or even overwhelming, will be ever less difficult.

Finally, this part is but an introduction to the endless and amazing promises God makes to those who love and serve Him. So, study your Bible daily, especially the words of Jesus Christ, and compile a list of additional promises. As you learn to live with these promises of God and Christ you will be astonished at the new strength and peace which will flood your life.

PROMISE 1

The Promise of Dynamic Life

I have set before you life and death ... therefore choose life, that both thou and thy seed may live: ... love the Lord thy God ... obey his voice, and ... cleave unto him: for he is thy life, and the length of thy days.

Deuteronomy 30: 19,20

God, our Creator, is also our Re-creator. So long as we are in unbroken contact with God the life force continues strong within us. But having the power of choice we may choose life or we may actually turn it off, depending upon how well we maintain spiritual contact.

When the life flow from God is reduced we run down in energy, health and power. But the recreative process or life renewal restores power and energy and it is not complicated. Simply love God, obey His voice, cleave unto Him. Then He will truly be "thy life, and the length of thy days."

Of Jesus Christ it was said, "In him was life," and Christ gives His own victorious life to all who live sincerely with Him. The basic method for constantly getting more out of life is simply to have more life within you.

PROMISE 2

God Will Always Be with You

As I was with Moses, so I will be with thee: I will not fail thee, nor forsake thee. Be strong and of a good courage . . .
                                                        Joshua 1:5,6

The greatest fact of all is that God is with us. We are not alone. He will never leave nor forsake us but will protect, guide and comfort us at any time, anywhere.

When the going is hard and you feel insecure and maybe fearful, just say this wonderful promise and remind yourself that He is always with you—always.

PROMISE 3

Hope for the Future

If my people, which are called by my name, shall humble themselves, and pray, and seek my face, and turn from their wicked ways; then will I hear from heaven, and will forgive their sin, and will heal their land.
                                                  2 Chronicles 7:14

The fear of world tragedy is deep in men's hearts. They hope and yet they fear. Catastrophe lurks in the dark shadows of impending nuclear war. Is mankind to burrow underground like animals seeking protection?

There is a better way. It is to accept God's great promise that if we turn humbly to Him He will hear our repentance and save us from disaster. He is our hope. As individuals we must turn to God and thus claim our part in the promise of mankind's salvation.

PROMISE 4

Good Things that Come to the Good Man

Blessed is the man that walketh not in the counsel of the ungodly, nor standeth in the way of sinners, nor sitteth in the seat of the scornful. But his delight is in the law of the Lord; and in his law doth he meditate day and night. And he shall be like a tree planted by the rivers of water, that bringeth forth his fruit in his season; his leaf also shall not wither; and whatsoever he doeth shall prosper.

Psalm 1:1-3

Good people have their troubles—there is no doubt about that. But by and large they have their reward too, and on earth as well as in heaven.

This promise tells us how to secure wonderful blessings. It is simply not to live in the company of sinful people. Do not become a cynic. Learn to love God's ways. Meditate upon and study His truth until your mind and heart are full of it.

Then your life will be blessed with richly creative values. All things will flow toward you rather than away from you. Your efforts will be blessed and God's bountiful prosperity will be yours. You will live on God's law of supply.

PROMISE 5

See God's Good in Difficulty

Behold, happy is the man whom God correcteth: therefore despise not thou the chastening of the Almighty: For he maketh sore, and bindeth up: he woundeth, and his hands make whole.   *Job 5:17,18*

God is trying to make men of us. The father who truly loves his son will not refrain from punishing when that is necessary to make a child stronger and wiser.

So when difficulties come, even painful ones, humbly receive them as a sign of God's deep favor. And remember if we are wounded He binds up and heals. God loves us like that; it is a man-sized love.

PROMISE 6

The Secret of Protection

He that dwelleth in the secret place of the most High shall abide under the shadow of the Almighty.   *Psalm 91:1*

This secret place might be described as religion in depth. Unhappily, not everyone finds this secret place, but anyone can. It does not require extra wisdom, certainly not any material possession. It requires only deep desire and complete surrender.

Live with God daily and you shall enter into the secret place of the most High, the deepest experience of life.

PROMISE 7

Forgiveness and Healing for You

Who forgiveth all thine iniquities; who healeth all thy diseases; Who redeemeth thy life from destruction ...
Psalm 103:3,4

The destructive forces of sin and disease do not necessarily go together—but sometimes they do and then they cause real trouble. Some spiritual persons, of course, suffer diseases in which sin is no factor at all.

God promises healing from both iniquity and disease. Those who accept true forgiveness are saved from the destruction of the soul. And those who are healed of disease attain that wholeness which God desires for each of His children.

PROMISE 8

How to Avoid Bad Happenings

The fear of the Lord tendeth to life: and he that hath it shall abide satisfied; he shall not be visited with evil.
Proverbs 19:23

The best kind of life comes to those who live with the fear of God in their hearts. By fear is meant awe, respect, veneration.

Such persons will try always to know and do God's will. That will mean self-discipline but it will result in self-mastery, one of the sweetest satisfactions in life. Such people, although they may experience difficulty and pain, will not suffer evil.

PROMISE 9

One Thing that Never Grows Old

The grass withereth, the flower fadeth: but the word of our God shall stand for ever.   Isaiah 40:8

As an old hymn expresses it, "Change and decay in all around I see. O thou who changest not, abide with me."

The years pass, loved ones go on ahead, papers yellow with age, the bloom of youth fades, white hair comes, changes follow one after the other and we sadly say, "Things are not as they were."

But one thing never changes because it is truth and truth is the same yesterday, today and forever.

So, let us cleave to that which never fades, never withers—the word of God that shall stand forever.

PROMISE 10

Abundant Blessings for You

Bring ye all the tithes into the storehouse, . . . and prove me now herewith, saith the Lord of hosts, if I will not open you the windows of heaven, and pour you out a blessing, that there shall not be room enough to receive it.   Malachi 3:10

This is one of the most often proved promises of God. And it never fails. Give God His Biblical share (at least one-tenth) and He will give you far more than your share. Indeed, He will overwhelm you with His blessings. Tithing is the stimulator of prosperity in all aspects of life, material and spiritual.

PROMISE 11

To Have Your Life—Give It

Whosoever will save his life shall lose it: and whosoever will lose his life for my sake shall find it. Matthew 16:25

This is a curious promise that runs counter to the modern materialistic conception that to have, one must get and keep. But for people who live only for themselves life shrinks and finally even withers.

But for those who give generously to help other people in Christ's name life grows ever richer. Lose yourself in big things outside yourself and you will find yourself. The more you give the more you receive from life.

PROMISE 12

The Reward of Endurance

But he that shall endure unto the end, the same shall be saved.   Matthew 24:13

Whoever embarks upon the Christian life will have periods of testing. However strong his faith he will experience down moments. He may see the things he believes in flouted. It may seem that Satan, not God, controls human affairs. He will not be spared opposition. He will be criticized, mistreated, misunderstood. The way will be far from easy.

When such times come, fall further back on God, pray more earnestly, surrender more completely.

PROMISE 13

Impossibles Become Possibles

And Jesus said unto them, . . . for verily I say unto you, If ye have faith as a grain of mustard seed, ye shall say unto this mountain, Remove hence to yonder place; and it shall remove; and nothing shall be impossible unto you.

Matthew 17:20

A mustard seed is very small but the point of this promise is that you do not need a big, well-developed faith to move mountainous difficulties. Just a little faith will do it but it must be the real thing, the kind that comes by deep desire and earnest prayer and disciplinary dealing with yourself.

Armed with this thoroughly genuine faith you can approach those huge difficulties and remove them. That which formerly seemed impossible becomes gloriously possible.

But it isn't you who shall remove big mountains of trouble from your path. It is rather your great faith—mountain-moving, mustard seed faith. Such faith changes hopeless impossibles into wonderful possibles.

PROMISE 14

Reward for Christian Witness

Whosoever therefore shall be ashamed of me and of my words in this adulterous and sinful generation; of him also shall the Son of man be ashamed, when he cometh in the glory of his Father with the holy angels.   Mark 8:38

All Bible promises are not gladsome. Some are pretty challenging, even stern. There is about them a rugged element.

This particular promise is a case in point. It is sharply directed to those who, while committed to Christ at least partially, try to keep it quiet so as perhaps not to disturb anyone or avoid seeming at all different from the nondedicated.

But no man can get away with such an all-things-to-all-men attitude. Christ insists upon courageous, all-out loyalty, even enthusiastic witness both by speech and action, particularly the latter.

And He promises that if our discipleship is not of the real variety He can hardly be expected to witness for us. We must have the character to stand up for Him in this pagan culture. Then He will witness for us at the final accounting.

PROMISE 15

The Quick Reward of Love

And he said unto Jesus, Lord, remember me when thou comest into thy kingdom. And Jesus said unto him, Verily I say unto thee, To day shalt thou be with me in paradise.   Luke 23:42,43

Through his pain the dying thief heard the jeers of the crucifying crowd. Pain often sharpens perception. Suddenly he knew that this noble character on the Cross was truly God's own Son. He believed and he humbly asked forgiveness and admission to God's Kingdom. No sooner was it asked than it was granted. So, too, when we believe and ask for pardon it will be granted. When our hearts accept Him Christ admits us to paradise.

PROMISE 16

The Promise of Everlasting Life

For God so loved the world, that he gave his only begotten Son, that whosoever believeth in him should not perish, but have everlasting life.   John 3:16

This is one of the most majestic of all Biblical promises. Jesus took upon Himself our guilt and atoned or paid with His own physical life for the wrong we have done. It represents God's supreme entreaty, His profoundest appeal to us. The great promise is that if we believe in the atoning power of Christ's death on our behalf we shall not perish when we die but have everlasting life.

PROMISE 17

No More Hunger or Thirst

And Jesus said unto them, I am the bread of life: he that cometh to me shall never hunger; and he that believeth on me shall never thirst.   **John 6:35**

The body must have food and water to live. Bread and water, therefore, are symbols of the deepest longing of mind and soul. Until that hunger and thirst are satisfied there can be no deep peace or joy. As Alfred Noyes says, "I am full-fed, and yet I hunger." When we surrender and truly accept Him by faith as Lord, then mind and soul hunger and thirst will be deeply and perpetually satisfied. Jesus Christ satisfies.

PROMISE 18

The Resurrection and the Life

Jesus said unto her, I am the resurrection, and the life: he that believeth in me, though he were dead, yet shall he live: And whosoever liveth and believeth in me shall never die.   **John 11:25,26**

This promise may be the most profoundly comforting statement ever made. Death of the body is the lot of all men, but through faith in Christ there need be no death of the soul.

When I first visited Bethany, the very spot where these immortal words were spoken by the Master, a warm feeling of assurance filled my soul. When the final day comes, put your hand in His and go forward unafraid.

PROMISE 19

Great Results of Faith

Verily, verily, I say unto you, He that believeth on me, the works that I do shall he do also; and greater works than these shall he do; because I go unto my Father. And whatsoever ye shall ask in my name, that will I do, that the Father may be glorified in the Son. If ye shall ask any thing in my name, I will do it.　　　　John 14:12-14

Here we are promised that our lives can demonstrate God's power and greatness. Even as Jesus Christ did great works of love, mercy and service, so can we also if we identify mind, heart and soul with Him.

So amazing is the operation of faith in the truly committed believer that anything he asks in the name of Christ will be given. This is, of course, no light or flippant promise, for to ask in His name means complete unselfishness and sacrificial spirit.

In His name desires are not material, save for basic need, but rather are spiritual.

In another passage it says: "God shall supply *all* your need."

So, therefore, in His name we may expect satisfaction of basic requirements. The great secret is to ask for that which He wants us to ask for. And it shall be granted overwhelmingly.

PROMISE 20

Troubles Can Be Overcome

These things I have spoken unto you, that in me ye might have peace. In the world ye shall have tribulation: but be of good cheer; I have overcome the world.   **John 16:33**

By "these things" is meant all the promises and commandments, Christ's whole message of love and salvation.

Believe these promises, live upon them and you shall have peace and assurance. And this even if the world is full of trouble.

Through faith in Him the world may also be full of the overcoming of trouble. So, regardless of difficulty be of good cheer, for victory is yours through Him.

PROMISE 21

Life, Energy, Completeness

For in him we live, and move, and have our being.
                                                   Acts 17:28

Life so easily runs down and becomes depleted. People say, "The life is knocked out of me."

But not when you live in Christ, for He is life itself. And when His vibrant life is within you it overcomes diminution and depression. Boundless energy is maintained so that you can move through your days with zest, vitality and a glorious sense of completion and fulfillment. Living with Him and in Him results in three great things: life, energy and wholeness of self.

PROMISE 22

The Wonderful Love of God

Who shall separate us from the love of Christ? shall tribulation, or distress, or persecution, or famine, or nakedness, or peril, or sword?

Nay, in all these things we are more than conquerors through him that loved us. For I am persuaded, that neither death, nor life, nor angels, nor principalities, nor powers, nor things present, nor things to come, Nor height, nor depth, nor any other creature, shall be able to separate us from the love of God, which is in Christ Jesus our Lord. Romans 8:35, 37-39

One thing the believer can always count on is the love of God as demonstrated in Christ. Know Christ, love Christ, follow Christ, cleave unto Him and the love of God will surround you all your life and beyond.

So great and so constant and unvarying is this love of God which we find in Christ that nothing of any sort, no matter how formidable, can separate you from it.

Tuck this tremendous promise close up against your heart, insert it deeply into your mind and never forget it. Keep close to Christ and His loving protection and help will follow you all the days of your life.

PROMISE 23

Don't Fear Old Age and Death

For we know that if our earthly house of this tabernacle were dissolved, we have a building of God, an house not made with hands, eternal in the heavens.

2 Corinthians 5:1

The physical body, the mortal house which your soul, the real you, uses as you live and work in this world will, like all material substances, gradually wear out.

Then you will move into another "house" in which the laws of materiality do not operate. Thus we have much to look forward to. Following God's laws we are building now our spiritual "house" for eternity.

PROMISE 24

If You Don't Tire of Doing Good

And let us not be weary in well doing: for in due season we shall reap, if we faint not.   *Galatians 6:9*

Evil doing can be awfully wearisome. In fact it produces a self-disgust that is most dissatisfying. And the good way of life has its hard moments too. It is not always easy to stay on a high level.

But God renews our hearts and keeps us going and holds us up. Indeed, He helps us to "mount up with wings as eagles" so that we shall run and not grow weary and finally can walk (when the going is hard) and not faint.

Just keep on keeping on in goodness. Stay with it and great blessing shall be yours.

PROMISE 25

God's Peace May Be Yours

And the peace of God, which passeth all understanding,
shall keep your hearts and minds through Christ Jesus.
                                                Philippians 4:7

If the peace of God passes all understanding so does it defy all description. We can only say that God's peace is an exalted feeling high above fears, irritations and conflicts. When it enters our hearts the old haunting fears give way to feelings of courage and confidence. The restlessness of life is quieted. What a promise! The ineffable peace of God offered by Christ is yours for the taking.

PROMISE 26

Reward of Defeating Temptation

Blessed is the man that endureth temptation: for when he
is tried, he shall receive the crown of life, which the Lord
hath promised to them that love him.   *James 1:12*

Temptation is the urge to do or say something wrong, something contrary to the will of God and the law of Christ. Temptation often comes in pleasant and seductive form and always the mind attempts to rationalize it, to make it seem all right.

If we endure and do not give in to evil we shall truly become master of life, ruler of ourselves. And Christ will help gain this victory.

PROMISE 27

The Victory of the Humble

God resisteth the proud, but giveth grace unto the humble. Submit yourselves therefore to God. Resist the devil, and he will flee from you. Draw nigh to God, and he will draw nigh to you. Cleanse your hands, ye sinners; and purify your hearts, ye double minded. Humble yourselves in the sight of the Lord, and he shall lift you up.

James 4:6-8,10

The proud and puffed up will have a hard time, for even God resists them. But he who humbly depends upon God will receive a vast strength.

Get close to God and God will be very near to you. Cleanse yourself of evil and get your thinking straight. Humbly admit your faults, ask God for strength and He will lift you up. Humbly follow Him and your life will be good, very good indeed.

PROMISE 28

Prayer Can Heal the Sick

And the prayer of faith shall save the sick, and the Lord shall raise him up.   **James 5:15**

I have personally seen this promise demonstrated many times. People who have been given up by doctors and loved ones have been raised up when someone has had enough faith to put them unreservedly into the hands of the Great Physician. There is tremendous power in the prayer of faith as applied in cases of illness.

PROMISE 29

God Will Forgive All Your Sins

If we confess our sins, he is faithful and just to forgive us
our sins, and to cleanse us from all unrighteousness.

1 John 1:9

You carry a heavy burden when sin is in your mind and
life. And since sin adds sin, the weight can break you. In
fact, many people live needlessly ineffective lives because
they won't let go the weight of sin.

But this relief-giving promise tells us that if we freely
confess to Him our wrongdoing and sincerely ask forgiveness, Jesus Christ will give new life to us. He is "faithful
and just" and will cleanse us from all evil.

PROMISE 30

Pray in Confidence for He Hears

And this is the confidence that we have in him, that, if we
ask any thing according to his will, he heareth us.

1 John 5:14

You can have complete confidence in the Lord and in
His promises. If you have His mind and talk His language,
possess His spirit, identify with His purposes, have His
love in your heart; if you are in His will He will always
hear you.

And God *does* always answer sincere prayer. He answers in three ways: (1) Yes, (2) No, (3) Wait awhile. And
every answer, whatever it may be, is for our good as long as
we are in His will.

PROMISE 31

The Final Glorious Promise

And I heard a great voice out of heaven saying, Behold, the tabernacle of God is with men, and he will dwell with them, and they shall be his people, and God himself shall be with them, and be their God. And God shall wipe away all tears from their eyes; and there shall be no more death, neither sorrow, nor crying, neither shall there be any more pain: for the former things are passed away. And he that sat upon the throne said, Behold, I make all things new. And he said unto me, Write: for these words are true and faithful. **Revelation 21:3-5**

In this world where there is so much trouble, so much pain, sorrow and death, those who believe on Him have a tremendous victory promised them. And this victory comes because we are His and He is ours.

So great is His love that He dries away human tears. No more shall there be death and crying. What a promise! By His vast power death itself is overcome. Everything becomes gloriously new.

This is perhaps the great and ultimate truth, that in Christ and God everything, both in persons and in the world, is changed; all becomes fresh and new and transformed.

Thus, the final glorious promise of God's goodness is the triumph of His love over pain and death.

PART TWO:

Enthusiasm!
The *Action* Handbook

A Word of Introduction

Because enthusiasm is so vitally important as a life motivation, we now offer ENTHUSIASM! *The Action Handbook*. And because enthusiasm makes a vast difference in one's life Emerson wrote: "Nothing great was ever achieved without enthusiasm."

Enthusiasm overcomes apathy, according to the famous historian Arnold Toynbee, who said, "Apathy can only be overcome by enthusiasm, and enthusiasm can only be aroused by two things; first, an ideal which takes the imagination by storm, and second, a definite intelligible plan for carrying that ideal into practice."

There is an extraordinary, dynamic quality about enthusiasm. It is permeated by a victorious attitude so powerful that it sweeps all before it. It brings the personality alive, releasing dormant powers.

Walt Whitman, great American poet, tells us that he found himself and set himself free through enthusiasm. He said, "I was simmering, really simmering; Emerson brought me to a boil." So many of us continue to simmer in our ineffectiveness until some profound motivation awakens us to the true possibilities inherent within us.

The difference between enthusiasm and faith is very slight indeed. Perhaps enthusiasm may be defined as faith that has been set afire. A pathetic fact is that not a few people go through their days without zest. There is little or no thrill to their lives. As a result they are sadly lacking in the power to meet and overcome difficulties victoriously. They age and grow old before their time.

Continuing vitality is dependent upon aliveness of spirit. Thoreau's warning should not go unheeded: "None are so old as those who have outlived enthusiasm."

May the following part of this book so stimulate enthusiasm that it makes a real difference in your life! And it can do just that. For it tells you how to have enthusiasm if you feel you are not an enthusiastic person. It also gives pointers on how to eliminate fear and worry through the practice of enthusiasm.

ENTHUSIASM! *The Action Handbook* describes how a dull job can become a fascinating daily experience as enthusiasm is applied. And the miracle-working power of enthusiasm in solving problems is opened to you. It tells how enthusiasm powers your self-motivating potential. In short, it will kindle within your mind and personality one of the greatest creative forces, the contagion of enthusiasm.

I assure you: if you will practice the principles of ENTHUSIASM! *The Action Handbook,* you will indeed change your life for the better.

ACTION STEP 1

Practice Enthusiasm and Have It

Eɴᴛʜᴜsɪᴀsᴍ is one of God's greatest gifts.

What is the outstanding characteristic of a little child? It is enthusiasm! He thinks the world is terrific; he just loves it, everything fascinates him. Huxley said that the secret of genius is to carry the spirit of the child into old age, which means never losing your enthusiasm. But all too few persons retain this excitement and a reason is they let enthusiasm be drained off. If you are not getting as much from life as you want to, then examine the state of your enthusiasm.

My own mother was one of the most enthusiastic persons I ever knew. She got an enormous thrill out of the most ordinary events. She had the ability to see romance and glory in everything. She traveled the world over. I recall one foggy night when she and I were crossing from New Jersey to New York City on a ferryboat. To me, there was nothing particularly beautiful about fog seen from a ferryboat, but my mother exclaimed, "Isn't this thrilling?"

"What is thrilling?" I asked.

"Why," she said, "the fog, the lights, that other ferryboat we just passed! Look at the mysterious way its lights fade into the mist."

Just then we heard the sound of a foghorn, deep-throated in the heavy, padded whiteness of the mist. My mother's face was that of an excited child. I had felt nothing about this ride except that I was in a hurry to get across the river.

She stood at the rail that night and eyed me appraisingly. "Norman," she said gently, "I have been giving you

advice all your life. Some of it you have taken; some you haven't. But here is some I want you to take. Make up your mind, right now, that the world is athrill with beauty and excitement. Keep yourself sensitized to it. Love the world, its beauty and its people." Anybody trying consistently to follow that simple course will be blessed with abundant enthusiasm and have a life full of joy.

"Miss Nobody"

One night I met "Miss Nobody." After a speech in a West Coast city a young woman gave me a limp handshake and said in a small, timid voice, "I thought I'd like to shake hands with you, but I really shouldn't be bothering you. There are so many important people here and I'm just a nobody."

"Please remain. I'd like to talk with you." Later I said, "Now, Miss Nobody, let's have a little visit."

"What did you call me?" she asked in surprise.

"I called you by the only name you gave. You told me you were a Nobody. Have you another name?"

"Of course," she said. "You see, I have quite an inferiority complex. I came to hear you hoping you might say something that would help me."

"Well," I answered, "I'm saying it to you now: You are a child of God." And I advised her to draw herself up tall each day and say to herself, "I am a child of God." I outlined for her some of the techniques in this booklet for practicing enthusiasm and self-confidence.

Recently, speaking in the same area, an attractive young woman approached. "Do you remember me? I'm the former Miss Nobody." Her enthusiastic manner and the sparkle in her eyes showed her change.

This incident underscores an important fact. You can

change! Anybody can change! And even from a dull nobody to an enthusiastic somebody.

Try the "As If" Principle

You can deliberately make yourself enthusiastic. To make yourself into whatever type of person you wish to be, first, decide specifically what particular characteristic you desire to possess and then hold that image firmly in consciousness. Second, proceed to develop it by acting as if you actually possessed the desired characteristic. And, third, believe and repeatedly affirm that you are in the process of self-creating the quality you wish to develop. In this way you use the "As If" principle.

William James, who taught this principle, said: "If you want a quality, act as if you already had it."

Shakespeare tells us in Act III of *Hamlet*, "Assume a virtue, if you have it not."

Frank Bettger, a top insurance man, was once dropped from a job for one reason only—lack of enthusiasm. "You must have enthusiasm. It's a primary requisite for success," he was told.

"But," complained Bettger, "what can I do? I haven't got enthusiasm. You just can't go out and buy it in a store. You either have it or you don't. I haven't, so that's it, I guess."

"You're wrong; make yourself act enthusiastic. It's as simple as that. *Act* with enthusiasm and soon you will *have* enthusiasm. Once you're fired with conviction your natural talents will take you to the top." And that is what happened to Frank Bettger, as he describes it in his famous book *How I Raised Myself from Failure to Success in Selling.**

*Prentice-Hall, Inc., West Nyack, New York 10994

Tell Yourself Good News

To develop enthusiasm, start the day right. You can condition a day in the first five minutes after you wake up. Henry Thoreau used to lie abed in the morning telling himself all the good news he could think of. Then he arose to meet the day in a world filled with good things, good people, good opportunities. The practice of spiritual motivation at the start of each day will infuse you with new zest.

The late William H. Danforth, a prominent business leader, said, "Every morning pull yourself up to your full height and stand tall. Then think tall—think great, elevated thoughts. Then go out and act tall. Do that and joy will flow to you."

Go on spreading enthusiasm all day, and at night you will have a deposit of joy in your life such as you never had before.

Read your Bible, for it is full of enthusiasm generators. What greater motivators, for example, are there than: "All things are possible to him that believeth" (Mark 9:33) and "Whatsoever ye shall ask in prayer, believing, ye shall receive" (Matt. 21:22)? Saturate your mind with great passages from the Bible.*

Then pray to God for guidance and get going!

Love Life and People to Be Enthusiastic

One magic formula for successful and enthusiastic living is stated in six powerful words: *find a need and fill it.* Every enterprise that has achieved success has been predicated on that formula.

Find people's needs, fill them. Love people. Love the sky, love beauty, love God. The person who loves always

*For forty life-changing Bible passages write to the Foundation for Christian Living, Pawling, NY 12564 and ask for my booklet *Thought Conditioners.* There is no charge.

becomes enthusiastic. If you're not enthusiastic, begin today to cultivate the love of living. Like Fred, for example, who runs a little eating place.

Resting a big hand on the counter, he asked me, "Okay, brother, what'll you have?"

"Are you Fred?"

"Yep."

"They tell me you have good hamburgers."

"Brother, you never ate such hamburgers."

"Okay, let me have one."

Along the counter was an old man who looked extremely miserable. He was sitting hunched over. His hand shook. After Fred had put my hamburger in front of me he went over and put his hand on that of this old fellow. "That's all right, Bill," he said. "That's all right. I'm going to fix you a bowl of that nice hot soup that you like." Bill nodded gratefully.

Another old man got up and shuffled over to pay his check. Fred said, "Mr. Brown, watch out for the cars out there on the avenue. They come pretty fast at night." And he added, "Have a look at the moonlight on the river. It's mighty pretty tonight."

When I paid my check I couldn't help remarking, "You know something, my friend? I like the way you spoke to those old men. You made them feel that life is good."

"Why not?" he asked. "Life *is* good. Me, I get a kick out of living. They're pretty sad old guys and our place is sort of like home to them. Anyway, I kind of like 'em."

Believe in yourself. Practice the principles of enthusiasm. Find needs and fill them. Believe that you can be better than you think you are. And remember—if you think you can, you can! Bring bona fide enthusiasm to your life style—for enthusiasm always makes the difference.

STEPS IN THE PRACTICE OF ENTHUSIASM

First: Act sensitized to the thrill of living.

Second: Hold the image of an enthusiastic you in consciousness.

Third: Practice the "As-If" principle—*act* as if you had enthusiasm.

Fourth: Start every morning with enthusiastic thoughts.

Fifth: Put vitality-activating Bible passages into your mind to spur your enthusiasm.

Sixth: Love life and people.

ACTION STEP 2

Enthusiasm Knocks Out Fear and Worry

A PHYSICIAN remarked that about half of the people who come into his office do not actually have anything physically wrong—they've just had the life knocked out of them and as a result have become prey to worries and fears. He said if only he could go to a shelf, get down a good bottle of enthusiasm, and inject a little of it into the bloodstream of these patients, he could restore their health and vitality. Fear and enthusiasm never mix.

Fear is Removable

A primary fact to know about fear is that it is removable. Fix that fact firmly in mind. Hold it tenaciously. No matter how many worries and anxieties harass you, remember always that they are removable. The medicine of enthusiasm, with its immense mental and spiritual power, can heal you of fear.

A good method of canceling out worry and fear is the deliberate use of enthusiasm plus self-discipline. As pointed out earlier, in order to have enthusiasm, simply act enthusiastic. Similarly, substitute enthusiasm for worry and fear, eliminating a destructive emotion in favor of a constructive one. A direct frontal attack on a personality weakness such as worry may be effective, especially if faith is emphasized. But in most cases an oblique attack, in the form of a substitute procedure or a psychological bypassing, is likely to get surer results.

Let us illustrate this anti-worry method with the history of a man who consulted me regarding an anxiety problem. In this man's mind was a strange conflicting mixture of anxiety-tinged ideas, which he feared yet didn't really believe in. But he did believe in them enough to be dominated by them. This attitude not only caused unhappiness, but also an enormous leakage of mental energy that might have been employed for constructive purposes.

I prescribed the oblique method of attacking worry. Rather than encouraging him to stand up to his anxiety, hitting it straight on as he bravely talked about doing, I said, "No, no, let's not do that. Let us outsmart your worry by coming at it from its blind side."

Five-Point Program for Attacking Worry

Specifically the method outlined was as follows:

First, he was to carefully practice listening to himself. He was to note and study with meticulous attention every comment he made, so that he might become fully conscious of the amazing number of doleful and negative remarks he was constantly uttering.

Second, he was to start being absolutely honest so that when he heard himself making a negative statement he was to ask himself: "Now look, do I honestly believe what I am saying or am I actually mouthing negativisms that I do not really believe at all?"

Third, he was to adopt the practice of saying exactly the opposite of what he usually said, and he was to note how much better the new affirmations sounded. As he continued this new procedure, it became ever more exciting to hear words and ideas full of life, hope and expectancy coming from his mouth instead of the old defeatist remarks. He soon discovered that something really exciting was happening to him, namely, an upsurge of dynamic enthusiasm.

Fourth, he was to keep track of everything that happened as he worked his new procedure, carefully noting and computing even the smallest results. If he had been, for example, in the habit of saying glumly: "Things aren't going to go well today," now (since he was no longer mouthing negativisms) he was to note that things were much better, as they usually are.

Fifth, he was to practice putting the best construction on every person and action each day. This is one of the most exciting of all personal development practices. I first came upon it through the late Harry Bullis, a leading figure in the flour-milling industry in Minneapolis. Harry was a genuinely enthusiastic man, so much so that I asked for an explanation of his happy nature. "I decided long ago," he said, "to put the best possible connotation on the words and actions of every person and every situation. Naturally I was not blind to the realities, but I always tried first to emphasize the best connotation, for I believe that such practice actually helps stimulate a good outcome. This best connotation practice resulted in enthusiasm for people, for business, for church and other interests, and greatly helped me toward a worry-free life."

The man to whom I gave this treatment had a remarkable improvement in his attitudes and life generally.

So in order to change the worry habit, first of all remember that persons can change—with determination and God's help.

Then as you speak and as you think, express only hopeful, enthusiastic ideas. Deliberately look at the best side and it will become natural to you to expect the good, the positive, the beautiful in life. You will automatically find in yourself the enthusiasm you desired. Express your enthusiasm freely and upon all occasions. You've got it made!

The Power of Affirmation

Another important technique in changing your outlook is that of affirmation. In fact, you can make almost anything of yourself by affirmation. Suppose, for example, you are full of fear. Say to yourself, "I'm not afraid. 'With God all things are possible' " (Matt. 19:26). The immediate effect may seem weak, but you will have taken the first step toward courage. And if you affirm it persistently enough, your conscious mind will accept this affirmation. Presently you will no longer be full of fear. Similarly, if you have been apathetic, but now start affirming enthusiasm, it will show in your new vitality. This requires self-disciplinary determination. It requires perseverance. But with the Lord's help you can achieve a new, positive attitude. "To become enthusiastic, ACT enthusiastic."

The Protecting Light of Enthusiasm

Driving one night in a country area, I noticed soft, yet efficient lights on poles near many of the farmhouses.

These were mercury-vapor lamps. They light up automatically at twilight, being triggered by the dark, and go off automatically at sunrise. The protecting light relieves the farmer's mind from fear of possible night intruders. Similarly, anyone who keeps the light of enthusiasm burning in his mind at all times dissipates that darkness of the mind in which fear grows. Remember, fear and enthusiasm simply cannot occupy the same mind at the same time. They are utterly incompatible.

A physician tells his patients to say their prayers and then to add "Good night, worries, see you in the morning."

As you develop real enthusiasm, worries and fears will no longer trouble you in the morning. You will be able to handle them. Never forget those tremendous words of Isaiah (35:4): "Say to them that are of a fearful heart, be strong, fear not."

STEPS IN DISPELLING FEAR AND WORRY

First: You became a worrier by practicing worry. You can become free of worry by practicing enthusiasm.

Second: Act enthusiastic to become enthusiastic.

Third: Practice saying something positive concerning everything and everybody.

Fourth: Never participate in a worry conversation.

Fifth: Replace gloomy fear thoughts with enthusiastic Bible passages. Make use of the power of enthusiastic affirmation.

Sixth: Cultivate friendships with enthusiastic persons.

Seventh: Help others to have an enthusiasm for life.

Eighth: Remember always that Jesus Christ is your partner. With Him all things are possible.

ACTION STEP 3

Change Your Job...with Enthusiasm

ENTHUSIASM is important to success. The president of a big company said, "If I am trying to decide between two men of fairly equal ability and one man definitely has enthusiasm, I know he will go farther, for enthusiasm has self-releasing power and carries all before it."

Certainly! A man with enthusiasm always wants to learn. He gives the job all he's got, throws everything into it. A man with enthusiasm is constantly releasing himself.

Learn to "Fail Forward"

The enthusiast has enormous resources that will equate with all problems. This does not mean that the enthusiast will not have his hard moments. He may even fail at times. Everybody does. But he learns something from failure. He "fails forward," and uses his failure creatively in the direction of eventual success.

You have heard the expression, "If life hands you a lemon, make lemonade." This is another way of saying, "fail forward." Enthusiasm keeps you from letting problems overwhelm you.

I know a man who manages a hotel. He so inspires his staff that all are vitally alive and enthusiastic. One day I was strolling with him along a path called "Philosopher's Walk."

"I like to take this walk," he said. "As a boy I worked in the kitchens of a large hotel in Chicago, so didn't get much schooling. But I learned to read such great thinkers as Marcus Aurelius, William James, Emerson, Socrates, Plato and, above all, Jesus. The hotel business can be very exasperating. But I found that if I fill my mind with such thoughts as those great men teach I can do my job and love it."

A few days later when a guest's bath overflowed and water came through the beautiful ceiling of the lobby, I found the manager pacing up and down Philosopher's Walk. "I am getting myself conditioned to talk to the lady who overflowed her bathtub," he explained.

When that woman left she asked to return the next year, saying she had never received such understanding treatment.

That man was able to maintain enthusiasm for his job with its exasperations through cultivated thought control. That happens when you develop a sense of enthusiasm for your job.

Give Yourself to Find Yourself

I spoke to two thousand men at a national convention of insurance agents. Seated beside the president of the association, I noted what a dynamic individual he was. He exuded energy, enthusiasm and vitality. I was greatly impressed, and asked him just how he came by all that aliveness.

"Five years ago I was a sleepy, unsuccessful life insurance agent. I was failing at everything. I was a member of our church back home, but I wasn't a good member.

"Then the pastor asked me to be chairman of the church finance committee. He sure was scraping the bottom of the barrel, because what did I know about church finances? I was failing in my own job and in financial difficulty personally. But for some reason the minister picked me. He told me the Lord had this job for me to do. That was the only time I had any doubts about Divine Wisdom. I said, 'Where am I going to get the information on what to do?' The pastor said, 'Read the Bible and do what it says.'

"To my surprise I found that the Bible is a great book on economics. It made me a tither—giving ten per cent of my time and money to the Lord. I recovered enthusiasm. My shattered personality came together. Everything changed for the better. That's why I'm so upbeat in spirit."

The more you give of yourself, the more you will find yourself. Give yourself to people. Pray for everybody. Give more time to the service of God and your fellow-man. Give of your money, of your life. Life will come flooding back to you, life and excitement such as you never felt before. Try it. It will work.

Let Go and Let God

The writer H.W. Arnold tells us: "The worst bankrupt is the man who has lost his enthusiasm. Let a man lose everything in the world but his enthusiasm and he will come through again to success." To keep full of enthusiasm, as God intended you to be, keep your intake of energy greater than the outgo of energy. If you are tense, uptight, the constant tension depletes you so that energy dissipates and with it your enthusiasm. Therefore, discover the great technique of being able to "let go and let God." Ask God for wisdom and guidance, and then give to your job the very best. Having done your best, leave the outcome to the Lord, trusting in His providence. You will find renewal, new energy, new enthusiasm.

Enthusiasm Changes Job Situations

Enthusiasm makes the difference in work performance. Expose your daily occupation to apathy, and your job will be difficult and tiresome. No job will go well for the person who considers it just another dull chore.

You may say, "My job is dull and has no future." But might it be that you have a dull attitude toward it? Try enthusiasm and watch it change. And see how you change with it. Enthusiasm changes a job because it changes the jobholder. When you apply enthusiasm to the job, the job comes alive with exciting new possibilities. So if you wish for a new job, try instead to apply enthusiasm to your present one that will make it new.

For instance, ask what someone else might see in your job. Consider what he or she would do with it. Perhaps that person is doing exceedingly well in his own work. Try to imagine what he would do if suddenly he took over your job. How do you think he would react toward it? What fresh and innovative changes would he make to put new life and achievement into what you consider a dull job? Then apply those ideas.

An employer told me he was going to fire a man out of the business. I asked, "Why not fire him *into* the business? Get him to try enthusiasm." He did, and the employee presently became an important man in the business. He was fired all right, but it was not out. Enthusiasm fired him to new participation. He became a new personality—successful, happy, creative. Try enthusiasm on your job. The result can be amazing.

STEPS TO PUT ENTHUSIASM INTO YOUR JOB
First: Remember that enthusiasm carries all before it.
Second: Learn to "fail forward."
Third: Find enthusiasm in Christ.
Fourth: Practice giving out and life will pour so much into you that enthusiasm will free your mind.

Fifth: Change your job by changing yourself into an enthusiastic person. Fire yourself *into* your job.

ACTION STEP 4

Enthusiasm Works Miracles in Problems

ENTHUSIASM is no simple, sweet or easy concept. It is a strong, rugged mental attitude that is hard to come by, difficult to maintain but powerful.

The word enthusiasm from the Greek *entheos* means God in you, or full of God. So when we claim for enthusiasm the power to work miracles in solving problems we are actually saying that God Himself in you supplies the wisdom, courage and faith necessary to deal successfully with all difficulties. We need only to discover how to apply efficiency and right thinking enthusiastically to our problems.

Attitudes Are More Important than Facts

Enthusiasm helps work miracles in problems because enthusiasm is an attitude of mind, and the mental attitude in a difficult situation is the important factor in its solution. Attitudes are more important than facts. Enthusiasm changes the mental outlook of fearing facts to the solid assurance that there is an answer.

One man looking at a tough problem says glumly, "There are the facts. There is nothing I can do but accept them." So the facts have him defeated. Another man, blessed with an enthusiastic attitude, seeing the same facts, says, "Sure, those are the facts all right, and they are indeed tough. But I never yet saw a set of difficult facts to which there was not a solution. Perhaps some facts cannot be changed, but maybe I can bypass or weave them into a new pattern or readjust my strategy. If necessary I can live with them and ultimately use them to advantage." That man's attitude brings the magic of creative believing into play.

These eleven words can make an amazing difference in your life: *Every problem contains within itself the seeds of its own solution.* The enthusiast described above knows this great truth.

Enthusiasm Equal to the Toughest Problems

In a western city two men took me to a prayer group meeting late one night. On the way one of them said, "A year ago we were a couple of drunks. But now we've got hold of something that has really changed us."

Some fifty people were gathered for the prayer meeting. They were sitting everywhere; three were even perched on the grand piano. A man was playing the piano and I'm sure he would have been a success in any nightclub. They were going from one hymn to another, singing until the sound threatened to raise the roof. Then all started to pray. A thrill like an electric charge went around among all the people during that prayer period.

A man and a woman stood up and testified: "We were breaking up our marriage. We were unfaithful to each other and we fought like cats and dogs. Now we love each other and we are sorry for what we were. But we have been lifted to a higher level."

"Who did this for you?" I asked.

"Jesus," they said, quietly.

Then a very beautiful woman stood and said, "I was an addict. I got so bad that one time I was picked up from the street where I lay in the gutter."

I exclaimed, "A beautiful girl like you?"

"Do you think so? It was Jesus who did it for me."

It was well after three a.m. when I got back to my room at the hotel and I had to catch an airplane at five o'clock. I did not go to bed at all that night. I did not need sleep. I was full of joy and energy and enthusiasm!

Such is the life that Jesus gives to people. There are those who make Christianity seem dull. It isn't that at all. It is free and untrammeled. It is life at its best. It bestows the priceless gift of enthusiasm, the life-changing power that enables you really to live.

A man I met at a convention remarked, "How can I learn the magic of believing—the power of enthusiasm?"

"Figure out a method of your own for practicing the magic of believing," I suggested. "You will find that it works and enthusiasm will be yours."

Here was his solution: Like many executives, he had on his desk a receptacle for incoming mail and other papers, and a second container for outgoing mail and papers. To this he added a third receptacle labeled, "With God All Things Are Possible." In this one he placed all matters for which he did not yet have answers and problems for which no solution had been determined. To use his own phrase, he held these matters in "prayerful thinking. I surround the problems in that box with the magic of believing and the results are amazing."

Use Self-Motivators

W. Clement Stone is a genuinely enthusiastic person. I asked him the secret of his enthusiasm.

"As you know," he answered, "the emotions are not always immediately subject to reason, but they are always immediately subject to action (mental or physical). Furthermore, repetition of the same thought or physical action develops into a habit which, repeated frequently enough, becomes an automatic reflex.

"And that's why I use self-motivators. A self-motivator is an affirmation that you deliberately use to move yourself to desirable action. You repeat a verbal self-motivator fifty times in the morning . . . fifty times at night . . . for a week or ten days, to imprint the words indelibly in your memory.

"Some self-motivators are:

- (Serious personal problem) *God is always a good God!*
- (Business problem) *You have a problem . . . that's good!*
- *Within every adversity there is a seed of an equivalent or greater benefit.*
- *What the mind can conceive and believe, the mind can achieve.*
- *Find one good idea that will work and . . . work that one idea!*
- *Do it now!*
- *To be enthusiastic . . . ACT . . . enthusiastically!*

"If a personal problem involves deep emotions, I always use man's greatest power immediately . . . the power of prayer. In solving business problems, I will also pray for guidance, but not necessarily immediately."

For Mr. Stone, enthusiasm makes the difference.

STEPS IN PROBLEM-SOLVING

Try these eight sure-fire guidelines with your problems:

First: Don't panic. Keep calm. Use your head. You'll need all your wits.

Second: Don't be overwhelmed by your problem. Don't get dramatic about it. Just tell yourself confidently, "God and I can handle it."

Third: Practice de-confusion. A problem generally becomes surrounded by confusion. So de-confuse it. Write down every facet of the problem.

Fourth: Skip the post-mortems. Don't say, "Why did I do that? Why didn't I do this?" Take the problem from where you now are.

Fifth: Look for a solution, not for the whole problem, but for the next step.

Sixth: Practice creative listening—to others through your outer ear, and to God through your deep inner ear.

Seventh: Always ask yourself what is the right thing to do in a given situation. Nothing wrong ever turned out right.

Eighth: Keep praying. Keep thinking. Keep believing. And keep enthusiasm going, for it works miracles in problems.

ACTION STEP 5

The Contagion of Enthusiasm

"ENTHUSIASM, like measles, mumps and the common cold, is highly contagious," says the writer Emory Ward.

But, unlike measles and mumps and colds, enthusiasm is good for you. Hope you catch it, and good.

When contagious, enthusiastic faith in yourself releases you from the self-built prison of your mind, then you begin to change, and as you change, your whole life changes also. Buddha said, "The mind is everything. What you think you become."

Perhaps you are being overwhelmed by your problems.

They have you disorganized and confused. There is Someone concerned about you. Jesus Christ will help you to turn about, march forward and win the battle. Heed His challenge, follow His leadership, and you will be filled with enthusiasm. And as you meet your problems they will give way before your enthusiasm and positive faith.

Enthusiasm Has Lifting Power

Let me tell you about one experience with the contagion of enthusiasm. As an introduction to my speech at a convention in Chicago, a skit was used.

The leading character was a businessman. In this little play he answered certain questions put to him by the others and at the same time gave a moving witness of what God had done for him. He told of the troubles he had faced in business; how life had become hard for him and he became nervous, tense and ineffective; how his doctor had finally told him he faced a nervous breakdown unless he could somehow find himself. Then he related how he had found God and Jesus Christ. In a simple, unaffected manner and in everyday, down-to-earth language he told how this wonderful thing had come into his life.

The room was filled with about four thousand people and it was late in the morning, after a number of speeches. Yet you could almost hear the stillness, you could feel the rapt attention.

I became aware of something coming up out of the audience, a lifting power, an indescribable, indefinable force, something intangible but very real, that had power in it. It held the quality of joy. It was deep, dynamic enthusiasm—an audience lifted and conditioned by a man's simple story of a tremendous spiritual experience.

Later in the day I met a physician who had been present

at this meeting. He remarked, "A strange thing happened. As I listened to that man I said to myself, 'This is a therapeutic thing. All unhealthy thoughts are being driven out of the minds of all these people. There is healing power in this place.'"

Zest for Life

We are meant to find zest for life even in the midst of its troubles.

In the office of a large business organization the head of the firm radiated exuberance and happiness. When I arrived he was with his chief assistant, and I listened to their conversation. The talk was positive and enthusiastic. It was a refreshing and stimulating and very upbeat conversation.

I sat back in my chair and said, "How do you explain such zest and optimism? You two are alive, really alive."

One of them leaned across the table and said, "Remember what Jesus said? 'These things have I spoken unto you, that my joy might remain in you, and that your joy might be full' (John 15:11). We believe in that teaching and take those 'things' seriously and practice them, so we get a thrill out of life and have a good time with our problems."

Those are men of influence who daily face problems, but they do so in a positive manner that seems to lift everything by a sheer infectious power. If you have zest and enthusiasm you attract zest and enthusiasm. Life does give back in kind.

"Let Enthusiasm Take Hold!"

I knew Vince Lombardi, fabulous football coach. When he came to Green Bay he faced a defeated, dispirited team. He stood before them, looked them over silently for a long time, and then in a quiet but intense way said, "Gentlemen, we are going to have a great football team. We are going to win games. Get that. You are going to learn to block. You are going to learn to run. You are going to learn to tackle. You are going to outplay the teams that come against you. Get that.

"And how is this to be done?" he continued. "You are to have confidence in me and enthusiasm for my system. The secret of the whole matter will be what goes on up here. [And he tapped his temple.] Hereafter, I want you to think of only three things: your home, your religion and the Green Bay Packers, in that order! Let enthusiasm take hold of you!"

The men sat up straight in their chairs. "I walked out of that meeting," writes the quarterback, "feeling ten feet tall!" That year they won 7 games—with virtually the same players who had lost 10 games the year before. The next year they won a Division title and the third year the World Championship. Why? Because, added to hard work and skill and love of the sport, enthusiasm made the difference.

What happened to the Green Bay Packers can happen to a church, to a business, to a country, to an individual. What goes on in the mind is what determines outcome. When an individual really gets enthusiasm you can see it in the flash of his eyes, in his alert and vibrant personality. You observe it in the spring of his step. You can see it in the verve of his whole being. Enthusiasm makes the difference in his attitude toward other people, toward his job, toward the world. It makes a great big difference in the zest and delight of human existence.

Are you alive? Do you have contagious enthusiasm? God the Father wants to give you the Kingdom, so that you will have super-delight in life. How is that done? By transferring life to you. Jesus said, "Because I live, ye shall live also" (John 14:19). And He meant abundant life, overflowing life. Because He lived it, you and I can live it too *if* we pay the price to get it.

STEPS TO CONTAGIOUS ENTHUSIASM

First: Like mumps, it can be caught, so expose yourself to enthusiastic people.

Second: Start thinking enthusiastic and positive thoughts about yourself.

Third: Let others catch enthusiasm from you.

Fourth: Know Jesus Christ—experience the vitality of His spirit.

ACTION STEP 6

Enthusiasm Can Remake Your Life

THE KIND of living that makes life good is as exact as a science, and not something that you just muddle through without following rules. Life responds to certain precise methods and procedures. Your life can be either a miss or a hit, can either be empty or full, depending on how you go at it. And the enthusiast knows and draws upon the resources. He plays it cool and straight. Finally, he believes there is nothing in life so difficult that it can't be overcome. This faith can move mountains. It can change people. It can change the world. You can survive all the great storms in your life.

However, enthusiasm is a quality that must be affirmed and reaffirmed. Donald Curtis suggests that you affirm each morning: "I move serenely forward into the adventure of life today. I am filled with inspiration and enthusiasm. I am guided and protected by the Infinite in everything I say and do. I project confidence and authority. I am sure of myself in every situation. With God's help, I am filled with the strength and energy to be what I am and to do what I have to do . . ."

Keep Enthusiasm and Nothing Can Break You

I once visited a brass foundry. A man showed me how they heated the molten brass to a temperature of 2,200 degrees Fahrenheit. It was heated in huge graflex crucibles. The intense heat made the whole crucible glow incandescently. Then, pointing to a crucible out of which this molten metal had only just been poured and which therefore was still red hot, the man said, "Let me show you something." He took an enormous sledge and, using all his force, smote this red-hot empty crucible again and again. The only effect was a few almost imperceptible dents, so resilient and resistant was the graflex at high temperature.

Then he showed me a crucible that had been allowed to cool and he took a small hammer, and with a flex of his wrist, hit this cold crucible a few times—and it shattered into a hundred pieces! "When it's cold," he said, "it's brittle.

"People are like those crucibles. When they are surcharged with spiritual fire and enthusiasm nothing can break them. But if they let the spiritual fire and enthusiasm die down, then even small blows of circumstance can crack and shatter them."

He Learned to Practice Enthusiasm

Suppose life has dealt harshly, and the zest, eagerness,

thrill and enthusiasm have gone out of you. How do you recover them? By one of the greatest devices God ever made—by rebirth. Down south one time I had dinner with a group of twenty men, ten ministers and ten laymen. One man in particular was a master storyteller. I remarked to the minister sitting next to me, "This character really has something."

"He surely has," the minister replied. "He's a member of my church. And he's my Exhibit A."

"What do you mean, 'Exhibit A'?"

"You should have seen him a few years ago. He was so gripey and crabbed, people avoided him. He had pains around the heart, he had pains up the arm, he was short of breath. He was a hypochondriac. And he haunted doctors' offices one after another. He took more pills than anybody in town. But they didn't seem to help him. He had built up a splendid business. Yet he was never happy.

"Finally a doctor shipped him off to a specialist in Chicago. And this Chicago specialist was a wise man. He told our friend, 'These pains of yours are pseudo pains. They do not come from any physical origin; they are induced by wrong, unhealthy thinking. Get your thinking changed, start living a vital, enthusiastic life—and you'll be well. That is my prescription. Fifteen hundred dollars, please.'

"Our friend exclaimed, 'Fifteen hundred bucks! For what?'

" 'For knowing what to tell you. You charge plenty in your business. So do I.' " (The doctor later explained he knew this man wouldn't value advice unless he had to pay for it.)

So this maladjusted man returned home and went immediately to his minister, saying, "That doctor in Chicago told me to get my thinking straightened out. You know, that fellow is a highwayman! He charged me fifteen hundred dollars! So how do I get my thinking straightened out? I'll get my fifteen hundred dollars' worth if it kills me!" (Which is precisely what the doctor had foreseen.)

The minister said, "Okay, Jim, how far do you live from here? Five miles? I see your chauffeur sitting out there in your car. Call him and dismiss him. I want you to walk home. And as you walk thank God for those feet of yours, thank God for your legs, thank God that you went to Chicago and were told you have a sound body. Walk home practicing enthusiasm for life, for yourself, for the pine forest you pass on the way, for all your friends, for your church, for God. And tomorrow, I want you to walk back here and tell me how you feel."

Eventually the man got wise and asked the minister to walk with him. The minister walked with him all in all a good twenty-five miles, until one day he challenged the man, "Why don't you let go and let the Lord Jesus Christ take over?" And he did.

"That is your storyteller," the minister told me in conclusion. "Exhibit A. He learned to practice enthusiasm and he is a well man—a happy man."

Every morning you have a new set of facts. Some of them are new forms of old facts. And that is what you have to work with. If you say, in the words of the Bible, "I will sing with the spirit, and I will sing with the understanding also " (1 Cor. 14:15), then you can take that set of facts and have the time of your life with them all day long.

Walk in Newness of Life

Maybe our forefathers grew great and strong because they drew strength from the sky and the hills and the streams—the forces and the wonders of nature. Enthusiastic men are men who live in relationship with nature and with nature's God. So activate your mind and let it flow out and become an alive part of the world. Thrill to the world, thrill to people. Heed the Bible, which tells us we should "walk in newness of life" (Rom. 6:4). That is a powerful idea. We're not supposed to be old, dead, dull, desultory. He who embraces the Gospel walks in newness of life. It is new every morning and fresh every evening.

The Bible positively glows with excitement and enthusiasm. It is the Book of Life. "Be renewed," it says in Ephesians 4:23, "in the spirit of your mind," not merely on the surface of your mind, but in the deep spirit that activates your thoughts.

Enthusiasm can remake your life!

EIGHT STEPS TO AN ENTHUSIASTIC LIFE

First: Stop running yourself down. There's a lot that's right in you. Empty your mind of your failures and mistakes and start respecting yourself.

Second: Eliminate self-pity. Start thinking of what you have left, instead of dwelling on what you have lost. List your assets on a piece of paper.

Third: Quit thinking of yourself. Think of helping others. Actually go out and find someone who needs the kind of help you can give and give it. For you will never have a continuing flow of abundance if your thought is only for yourself.

Fourth: Remember Goethe: "He who has a firm will molds the world to himself." Almighty God put a tough thing into human beings called the will. Use it.

Fifth: Have a goal and put a timetable on it.

Sixth: Stop wasting your mental energy on gripes and postmortems, and start thinking about what to do now. Amazing things happen when you think constructively.

Seventh: Every morning and every evening of your life articulate these words: "I can do all things through Christ who strengthens me" (Phil. 4:13).

Eighth: Every day three times say: "This is the day the Lord has made. I will rejoice and be glad in it" (Psalm 118:24).

PART THREE:

You Can Overcome Any Problem!

An *Action* Manual

A Word to the Reader

PROBLEMS are never in short supply. But today they seem accentuated both in number and intensity. An old spiritual says "nobody knows the trouble I've seen." Similarly, we often feel that nobody suffers the difficulties that throng about us and harass us.

This part is designed to offer suggestions not merely to help you meet and endure difficulties. It's much more than that. It is an *action* section. And its purpose is to show you how to overcome your problems . . . and overcome them now. It's an *overcome now* formula.

A young man whom I once met in an airport told me: "I've got plenty of problems. But don't do any worrying about me. God and I together can handle all difficulties. Be seeing you." And he walked off jauntily! It was evident that he had the components of the answer. He was thinking right; he faced his problems, and he had God going with him. And, I may add, so have you.

We shall outline a series of steps together with specific techniques that will work when worked, and with these you can make real progress in overcoming your problems. That is, if you will start, continue and not lose patience in the process. There will, of course, be times of discouragement, times when it seems no progress is being made. But keep thinking positively, stay with the effort and follow the suggestions given. I am sure you will overcome your problems because others have done so by following the action formulas suggested here.

STEP NUMBER ONE

Think Positively

AT THE very beginning of your effort to overcome your problems it will be necessary to take a positive mental attitude toward them, to think and believe that you can master them and that indeed you are now proceeding to do so. Do this and the action has begun.

In my office is a sign someone made for me. It reads "Attitudes are more important than facts." That legend has proved helpful in handling my own problems because it teaches how to look at a fact. The negativist may say, "Here is a hard, tough fact. You just can't get around a fact. A fact is a fact and that is that."

But the positivist on the other hand says, "Yes, it is a fact. That must be recognized. But there is a way to deal with this or any fact: go around it or under it or over it or hit it straight on. A fact is for solving and I've got what it takes to do just that."

The negativist is likely to be defeated by the fact, while the positivist will probably handle it creatively. It is not so much the fact as your attitude toward the fact that determines the outcome.

How you think about a problem is the issue of paramount importance. You can think yourself to success, or you can think yourself to failure. You can think yourself to victory over your problems, or you can think yourself to defeat by them. The kind and manner of your thoughts determine the eventual results you will experience.

There is a law called the law of attraction. Like attracts like. "Birds of a feather flock together." Thoughts of a kind have a natural affinity. So therefore the negative thinker sending forth negative thoughts, stimulating the world around him negatively, draws back to himself, in the very nature of the case, negative results. That which you yourself send out in the way of thought is bound to come back to you.

The positive thinker on the other hand sends out of his brain positive, optimistic, faith-filled thoughts. He activates the world around him positively. On the basis of the same law of attraction he tends thereby to draw back to himself positive results.

Consider the case of two salesmen. One was assigned territory which had produced very little business for the company. This territory had the reputation that "nobody can do anything with it."

This man went to his new territory in full acceptance of the general appraisal that there was no business possibility there. "So," he reasoned, "why knock myself out? I am being unfairly treated by having this non-producing area hung around my neck." You will not be surprised to know that he failed to develop any appreciable amount of new business and left the company. He never even gave it a try. It was for him a fact that no opportunity was available there. His attitude toward it was negative. Results? Negative!

A second salesman, brought in from across the country, knew nothing about the territory except that it was centered around a thriving metropolitan community. No one had told him that it contained no sales possibility, so he proceeded to get busy and make many sales. "Why, this is an unworked gold mine!" he exclaimed. All his thinking was positive and his activity was positive. He made a great success of the territory. But so profound was this man's positive mental attitude that had anyone told him it was a bad territory he wouldn't have believed it. And why should he? There were hundreds of thousands of people living there and they needed his product and he was there to see that they had it. He was a successful man.

You can think your way through and finally out of any difficulty or problem. But you must think, not react emotionally. When a difficulty strikes, the tendency is to panic or to be upset, even to be resentful. Such reactions are emotionally conditioned, and if one's acts are determined in such a state of mind they are likely to be lacking full rationality.

One must discipline himself to be calm in his thinking. He must cool it. For the mind cannot think when it is hot; only when the mind is cool will it produce those rational factual concepts which lead to solutions. So do not allow yourself to emote. Think!

Actually, your head is your greatest asset. Keep it always under disciplinary control. Remember the statement credited to Thomas A. Edison, "The chief purpose of the body is to carry the brain around." The great inventor knew that it is in the mind, working in non-overheated fashion, that we get ideas, not impulses. And with these sound ideas we solve problems.

ACTION FORMULA

1. Take a positive mental attitude toward any problem.

2. Stop all negative thought, all negative talk.

3. Affirm that your attitude toward a fact is more important than the fact.

4. Emphasize the law of attraction. Attract by your positive thinking only positive results.

5. Discipline yourself to keep your mind always calm and untroubled. Cool it.

STEP NUMBER TWO

Believe Your Way Through

Make it your action now to develop a real faith in God and in yourself. With that faith you can believe yourself right through your problem.

J.C. Penney, the famous merchant, a longtime friend of mine, lived a vigorous 95 years. We were seated together at the speaker's table in the Grand Ballroom of the Hotel Waldorf-Astoria in New York and fell to discussing problems and what to do about them. "You have had plenty of difficulty in your long lifetime, J.C.," I said. "What is your philosophy of a problem?"

His answer was characteristic of this great and good man. "Well, Norman," he replied, "actually I'm grateful for all my problems. As each of them was overcome I became stronger and more able to meet those yet to come. I grew on my difficulties."

Believe you can and you can—this dynamic principle has been demonstrated in the lives of too many believers to leave any doubt concerning its validity. It is very important to believe that you can, with God's help, meet and overcome all problems. And the more profoundly you believe, the more surely you will gain victory. The words *believe* and *can* are linked together in a creative action unity. If you believe you can, you can.

The Bible bears out this truth when it says, "If thou canst believe, all things are possible to him that believeth" (Mark 9:23). A man who had been experiencing one failure after another saw in a book a phrase that gripped him. It was this: "Expect the best and get it." It hit him hard and he admitted to himself that he had been thinking defeat thoughts. At once he realized he had been proving the Scripture in reverse. Every day he had been expecting the worst and usually getting it.

So he began searching through the Bible for more such "practical" ideas, the kind that would make a believer of him and erase his failure image. He found many, including these two.: "Ask, and it shall be given you; seek, and ye shall find; knock, and it shall be opened unto you" (Matthew 7:7), and "For God hath not given us the spirit of fear; but of power, and of love, and of a sound mind" (2nd Timothy 1:7).

These Scripture ideas did a real mind-washing job on him, cleaning out the doubts and inferiorities. "I decided," he said, "to take a different attitude toward my job. I would start out each morning saying, 'I like my job. This is going to be the greatest day of my life.' Before long, these words, repeated over and over, started to become reality. I began to see that if I did not believe in myself I could not expect anyone else to believe in me." Such was the experience of R. Gene Scalf, who told in *Guideposts* how he learned to believe his way through problems.

So, if you want to become a believer with vital-action faith, start buttressing your weak faith with the powerful concepts of the Bible. The Bible is packed full of faith-producing thoughts that can revamp your mental attitude. Take them into your conscious mind by reading. Then commit them to memory, thus holding them firmly in mind. Finally, by a process of spiritual and mental osmosis they will pass deeply into the subconscious, and when that happens you will become a believer who can believe your way through your problems. And remember this, "If ye have faith as a grain of mustard seed, ye shall say unto this mountain, Remove hence to yonder place; and it shall remove: and nothing shall be impossible unto you" (Matthew 17:20).

Let me tell you of another man. His name was Fred Haas, one of those rare believers who is made by all-out faith. He believed his way gloriously through a mass of problems.

After 30 years of hard work Fred lost his business because of a crooked partner. I expected him to be full of bitterness when he came to see me. Instead, he told me that he had found his assets to be much greater than his liabilities.

"All I had when I began thirty years ago was $50. Now I have $500, so, you see, I'm ahead on that," he said with a grin. "I started with a wonderful wife, and I still have her, thank God. And I'm way ahead on experience."

Within a year after this setback he had gotten another business started and was doing well. But the statement he made which really stayed with me was this: "I decided I would not be an *if* thinker, but a *how* thinker."

That's really quite a thought-provoking distinction. The *if* thinker broods over a difficulty or a setback, saying bitterly to himself, "If only I had done thus and so. . . . If only this or that circumstance had been different. . . . If others had not treated me so unfairly. . . ." So it goes from explanation to explanation, round and round, getting nowhere. The world is full of defeated *if* thinkers.

The *how* thinker, on the other hand, wastes no energy on post-mortems when trouble or even disaster hits him, but immediately starts looking for the best solution, for he knows there always is a solution. He asks himself, "How can I use this setback creatively? How can I work something good out of it?"

The *how* thinker gets problems solved effectively because he knows that values are always inherent in difficulty. He wastes no time with futile *ifs* but goes right to work on the creative *how*.

The next time trouble strikes you, avoid the word *if*. Focus on the dynamic word *how*. Then ask God's help to put know-how into the how. You will be amazed at how quickly your problems will be resolved.

One reason the believer successfully believes his way through problems is that he never runs away. He is not so superficial and foolish as to think that if he can just run out on his present difficulties things will be easier elsewhere. He knows that the same or similar difficulties will follow him wherever he goes, and that the only sure way to stop running is to stand up to those problems right where he is and fight the battle. And this applies to all of us. If you do not defeat problems right here and right now, they will chase and hound you the rest of your life. Don't run; fight it out, believe it through—now, and right where you are. That is the formula that works with that phenomenon called a problem.

I met a young man who positively exuded dynamic confidence. He was in sales and it was evident that he was literally bursting with enthusiasm for his job and for salesmanship generally. "I love to sell," he declared. "I just love it. There is nothing like the challenge and excitement of selling." He was most impressive and inspirational.

But he admitted that he had not always had this positive mental attitude and undefeatable spirit. Far from it. Formerly he was afraid to call upon a potential buyer. To make a "cold" call practically terrified him. So overwhelmed was he that he would lie on a couch in his home afraid to go out to do his job. He alternately went hot and cold and literally cowered with fear. He was completely defeated. And yet, really he wasn't because he continued to think and pray. As a result, an idea came which saved him.

Being very personable, he was offered a job by another organization—a job much easier than his selling job. He was delighted and terribly relieved. Even at the start, this new job would net him twice the amount he was currently making. What a wonderful out. He could escape this sales job which frightened him so much.

But the idea that saved him from making a mistake, the idea that came through thinking and praying, was that running never got you anywhere except into more running. If he did not win the battle with fear right where he was, fear would follow him wherever he went, however inviting a new job seemed.

So he asked the Lord's help. He stood up to his fears. He refused to run. He declined the attractive job opportunity. He decided he would "fight the good fight, finish the course, and keep the faith." God gave him the strength that He always gives to anyone who believes. The young man conquered his fears. He not only learned to sell, he learned to love it. And a few years later the company whose job offer he had declined offered him an even better position.

So, never run from difficulties. Believe your way through them. And you can if you believe you can. God is always standing with you, and His help never fails.

ACTION FORMULA
1. Believe in God.
2. Believe in yourself.
3. Grow strong on your problems.

4. Believe you can and you can.
5. Saturate your mind with faith from the Bible.
6. Don't be an *if* thinker. Be a *how* thinker.
7. Never run from a problem—stand up to it.

STEP NUMBER THREE

Learn Know-How from Your Problems

DON'T fight a problem. And never complain when a problem strikes you. Instead, start asking questions of the problem. For it is full of know-how for you. Actually, a problem is one of God's greatest methods for teaching you, for helping you to develop.

Charles F. Kettering, famous research scientist, was a wise man, a kind of natural-born philosopher. He was an inventive genius of high order, especially in the automotive field. I had a most illuminating conversation with this great thinker in the course of which he expounded his philosophy on problems. "I could do nothing without problems," he declared emphatically, "they toughen my mind. In fact," he said, "I tell my assistants not to bring me their successes, for they weaken me; but rather to bring me their problems, for they strengthen me."

When a problem comes along, instead of bewailing and complaining, just say to God, "Lord, what are You trying to teach me by this problem? What insights do You wish to give me?" Then tackle the problem, using all your thought power and prayer power. Some of the most amazing guidance you will ever experience will come to you as you crack open a problem. You will then have the know-how to overcome it.

People sometimes ask, "Why must we have so many problems? Wouldn't life be simply wonderful," they say, "if we had fewer problems or easier problems or, better still, no problems at all?" This attitude is based on the widely held assumption that there is something inherently bad about a problem. But, on the contrary, may it not be true that a problem can be a very good thing? May it not be filled with possibility and potential?

Would you actually be better off if you had fewer problems, or easier problems or no problems whatsoever? The answer is that those who have no problems are in the cemetery. For them life's fitful fever is over; they rest from their labors. They couldn't care less about all that goes on in this life. They have no problems at all; but they are dead. It follows therefore in logical sequence that problems constitute a sign of life. Indeed, the more problems you have, the more alive you are.

So, rather than complaining, be glad that you have problems, for it means you are alive and vital and that God believes you possess the ability to handle problems. And this booklet is designed to help you to do just that.

Look at every problem as containing some amazing value for you. When God wants to give you something of great worth, does He present it on a silver platter as something that comes easy? Not often. He is more likely to bury it at the core of a tough, hard problem. That precious value may be difficult to come by but if you view every problem as a value container rather than something to harass you, the result will be greater knowledge and achievement than ever before.

Some years ago I knew an inspirational man who taught

me the technique of looking for "the pearl of great price" buried at the heart of a problem. As a young man burdened by a seemingly insoluble problem I went to him for advice. "So you've got a problem," he said. "Congratulations!"

"How come congratulations?" I asked in surprise. Sympathy seemed more in order. "Because," he replied cheerfully, "out of this problem some big wonderful thing may come into your life."

At his encouragement I outlined the problem in full detail. He listened carefully as I laid the entire problem out before him. "There it is, this big problem of yours. Now what do we do? First, let's not be afraid, certainly not be awed by it. The face of it is not grim. Actually it is smiling at you, asking that you play hide and seek with it. There is something great hiding in it. The fun is for you to find it. Something God put there in that problem is for you and God gave you the brains to think it through and to find know-how within it."

Whimsically be began poking with his forefinger at an imaginary mass laid on the table. "Every problem has a soft spot," he explained. "We'll find it." Presently he chuckled, "Here it is. Now let's start breaking this problem apart. I'm sure we will find something wonderful in it." And under his skillful guidance we did find one of the greatest values in my personal experience. I have had profound respect for problems ever since, knowing that each one that comes my way may come bearing a priceless gift of know-how, insight and understanding.

If you approach a problem spiritually with full mental effort and then add a genuine faith, insights and guidance will be given you amazingly. You may actually receive specific direction. God will show you what to do about your problem. You will be given great power over it. But how can you know what steps to take, what decisions to make, which way to turn? There are several ways, but one is the method of the "closed doors."

My mother used to tell me, "When a door slams shut in your face it's just God guiding you further along to an open door He has for you." I personally found that belief in this principle and long-time application of it gave me victory over disappointment and apparent defeat. I went forward confidently toward the open door.

So be grateful for your problems. They are full of values for you if you believe.

ACTION FORMULA

1. Don't fight a problem. Always ask questions of it. Ask, "What is God saying to me in this problem?"

2. Be glad you have problems for it proves you are alive.

3. Believe that a problem is not inherently bad but good.

4. See buried in every problem an amazing value for you.

5. Approach every problem with a think–pray–believe formula.

6. Go forward on the amazing closed–door, open–door technique.

STEP NUMBER FOUR

You Are Bigger Than Your Problem

IN THE process of overcoming any problem it is important to have a proper appraisal of yourself in relation to the problem. And the truth we want to emphasize with all force and sincerity is that you are bigger than your problem. And that goes for any issue you will ever be called upon to face. So now affirm strongly and believe it: "I am bigger than any problem. I can overcome any problem." Do not doubt, for your affirmation is sound and true.

The basis for this confidence in yourself is that you are a child of God, created in the Divine Image. No group of factors can match such a relationship: you and the great God your Creator. When God made you He made you great. He made you strong like Himself. Practice believing this until you accept it fully in the depths of consciousness and you will presently come to know for certain that you are bigger than your problem.

Our tendency often is to feel inferior and inadequate in the presence of a problem. We may even be obsessed with a haunting, conflicted sense of our inability to cope with the problems of human existence generally, and with the present problem in particular. In the mind one tends to blow the problem up in imagination to an extent that is out of all proportion to its actual size. It scares and frightens not because it is too big for us but because our fearful thoughts have invested it with a difficulty that it does not really possess.

An important procedure then is to cut the problem down to its true proportions; reduce it to size. Empty out the fear-panic-inadequacy feeling and start thinking with objective rationality. See the problem straight. Defuse emotional reactions. Activate creative thought.

In a business office I found a man behind a desk on which sheets of paper all of a size were laid out in orderly pattern. Each sheet contained handwritten notations. This man said, "You may be curious about what goes on here with these papers. Actually I'm dealing with a pretty big and rough problem. And I have my own way of doing that."

He went on to tell me that there was a time in his life when he was "licked" by a problem and, in fact, was dismayed when he was called upon to face one. Usually the problem seemed overwhelming. Then he met an older businessman who said, "Look, Jack, I've found that usually no problem is as forbidding as it seems. I discovered that if you begin taking a problem apart, breaking it up into its component parts, you can handle the whole problem by dealing with those parts separately. Take a problem in bits and pieces. You can handle them by that method. And the bits and pieces will add up to handling the entire problem. Try this way and the matter won't look so big to you."

"That advice made sense," my friend said, "so my method is what you see here. I thoroughly analyze the problem, breaking it up and writing on these papers its various aspects. Then," he continued, "I pray and ask for guidance as to how to proceed. Usually I gain an insight from the prayer, as a result of which I select one element of the problem with which to begin.

"I 'chisel' off the easiest part first and dispose of that. In this manner I continue to work and pray until the problem is reduced to its central core. Then it's wonderful how adequate I feel in dealing with the essence of the matter. This method really works," he declared enthusiastically, "so much so that I'm getting a greater kick out of life than ever. I've found that I am bigger than any problem," he concluded stoutly.

So never let any problem overawe you. You are bigger than it is. You have the mental and spiritual power to overcome it. Take the problem calmly and confidently as it comes. Never depreciate yourself or emphasize your limitations. Many defeated persons are defeated simply because they are "self-limitators." Their self-image causes them to see themselves as weak and incompetent. You are what your self-image is. So begin changing your self-image. Cast off the self-limiting concepts which are rendering you ineffective. Be what you really are—a child of God, unlimited, free and great, really great. Start being that now in your mind and presently you will be that in fact.

One of the greatest gems of wisdom ever given me was a statement by a life-long friend, Rob Rowbottom. A man of strong faith, a true child of God, he said, "Never build a case against yourself." So utterly right, so profoundly powerful is that insight that you would do well to write it on a card. Carry it in your wallet. Paste it on your mirror. Slip it under the glass top of your desk. Tack it above the kitchen sink. But better still, imprint it in consciousness until it really takes hold and starts motivating you. It's simply terrific! It's wonder-working! "Never build a case against yourself."

And what does it mean? Simply this: That no longer are you going to tell yourself what you can't do, that you are an inferior person lacking in ability, not capable of overcoming your problems. From now on you are striking the "t" off that word "can't" so that it stands out clear and strong, "I can because I am." Am what? A child of God, one who is intended not to be defeated by life but to master it.

And to fortify your upgraded spirit, your changed attitude, your new self-image, imprint on your mind another statement, that great and glorious affirmation, "I can do all things through Christ which strengtheneth me" (Philippians 4:13).

Turn your former self-limiting concepts into self-creating factors. Like Tom Dempsey, for example.

Some years ago this remarkable football player, Tom Dempsey of the New Orleans Saints, single-handedly won a game over the New York Giants. He was considered by some to be the greatest field-goal kicker in the game. With unerring accuracy he would boot the ball right over the crossbar. He kicked a record 63-yard field goal, breaking the previous record by 7 yards. He was a genius with the foot—and that is because he was also a genius with the mind.

His foot was motivated by a positive mental attitude, for Tom Dempsey, big, husky chap that he is, was born with a half-formed right foot. He had to wear an orthopedic kicking shoe that cost $200. But with that half foot he made these stellar kicks.

And that isn't all of it. Tom Dempsey was born with a right hand that has no fingers. Now how in the world are you going to play football with a half foot and a hand that has no fingers? The way you do it is to believe that you can do it! One sportswriter asked him, "How do you do so well being handicapped?"

He replied, "I don't know that word. I never thought of myself as being handicapped. And as for the word *can't*, it doesn't exist in my vocabulary."

Don't let it exist in *your* vocabulary, either. You are bigger than your problem, and that goes for whatever your problem may be.

ACTION FORMULA

1. Get a right appraisal of yourself in relation to your problem.

2. Affirm and do not doubt. "I can overcome any problem

because I'm bigger than it is."

3. Every day say, "I am a child of God."

4. Cut every problem down to size. Chip off the easiest elements first until you can handle the problem's core.

5. Never let any problem overawe you.

6. Do not depreciate yourself. Impose no self-limitations.

7. Never build a case against yourself.

8. Build up your self-image.

9. Throw the word "can't " out of your vocabulary.

STEP NUMBER FIVE

God Is with You

Believe that God is with you, for He is. "I am with you always," promise the Scriptures.

When we assert that you can overcome any problem, we are taking into account that you do not have to do it entirely on your own. For, you see, God is with you. You have big extra help available from Him. Thus, you have the advantage of insight and strength greater than any human being possesses. What problem can possibly be too much for God and you acting together in perfect harmony? It's the greatest combination of all.

An attractive young wife glowingly told me of the many ways in which God had been with her in problems. And she had plenty of problems. Among other difficulties, she had been crippled by infantile paralysis. But the victorious spirit so evident within her demonstrated that she knew how to overcome any problem.

"What is your secret?" I asked admiringly.

"Oh," she declared excitely, "I have God's telephone

number. I can call Him anytime. And His line is never busy. He always answers."

"And what is God's telephone number?" I asked.

"It's Jer 33:3. That is Jeremiah, Chapter 33, verse 3, where it says, 'Call unto me, and I will answer thee, and show thee great and mighty things, which thou knowest not.' "

Certainly you can handle any and all of your problems if you have "God's telephone number," knowing that Divine counsel and help are always readily available.

If problems seem too much for you, perhaps it is because you are not calling upon God. His phone is not disconnected. Nor is the line busy. He is right there waiting to hear from you. Dial His number (Jer 33:3). Call upon Him and He will answer you at once. He will show you a way out of your difficulties. He will guide you in overcoming any problem. Get firmly fixed in mind the great fact that God is with you—always with you.

And how can you be sure that God is with you personally—and very near, at that? One method is to practice God's presence. Talk with Him in the mind, think with Him. Try to act like Him, making every effort to conduct yourself as you believe God wants you to live. Constantly employ the assumption that God is at your side, indeed even nearer than that. He is within your very nature. In due course the assumption will give way to certainty of the fact. You will know without any doubt whatsoever that the Presence is real, completely valid.

A man consulted me once who dismally complained that he was overwhelmed by problems and couldn't see his way through them. Knowing this man quite well, I was aware of the quality of his mind. While at the moment his thoughts were under a heavy cover of dark clouds, I was sure that he possessed the capacity to believe. I had confidence that he would be able to believe his way out of this gloomy mental overcast.

My suggestion to him was that he practice the presence of God in every way possible. He was to talk to God as he drove his car. Walking along the street, he was to affirm that God actually walked with him. In a restaurant, if he could unobtrusively do so, he was to pull alongside an empty chair for the Lord. And at night he was to have an empty chair by his bed. The objective was to effect, through such practice, a mental attitude that would develop a faith far greater than his problems.

I must say that this man really went all out in objectifying the Divine Presence. It became an integral part of his daily routine, so much so that one night, waking out of sleep, he placed his hand on the nearby chair and actually "felt" that his hand was grasped.

"Of course, my mind could have been playing tricks on me," he said. "But I don't believe it. I know for a fact that He was there by my bed. And I can tell you why I'm so certain. It's because now those problems no longer lick me at all. I'm on top of them. I know that God is with me because things go easier. And those dark clouds have lifted off my mind."

So the suggested action is to practice the Presence in whatever way may seem most meaningful. This practical activation of faith, this objectifying of belief, manifests itself in a convincing actuality of God as with you, helping you. And with it you are equal to any problem. Try it and discover this great fact for yourself. Get with it. Get with God.

Often it has been demonstrated that the thought of God activates forces which so completely revolutionize persons that problems which formerly defeated them are overcome by the power of the God thought. This thought of God has shown itself able to cut through a mass of defeat attitudes and let in the clear and healing light of truth.

Take the well-known singer, Johnny Cash, as an example of this process. According to a magazine article, he woke up one morning in jail. He was not there for any misdemeanor, but for his own protection. He had been on pills, "looking for peace." He admits that he became afraid of everything. Before a performance he was a nervous wreck, sometimes almost too sick to work. Sometimes he did not even appear for a scheduled show. Now here he was lying on a jail cot staring at the ceiling.

"I'm a fan of yours, Johnny," said the elderly jailer. "It's a shame to see you ruining yourself. I didn't know you were this bad off." As he opened the door for the singer the old man continued, "Your great talent came from God. You're sure wrecking the body He put it in."

As Cash stepped into the warm sunshine the word "God," dropped by the jail keeper, kept reverberating through his mind. Until then it had never occurred to him that God could or would help him with his problem or give him the strength to kick his habit. He realized that to be free he would have to have help. "I asked God to go to work on me right then and there," he said later. Needless to say, he fought the battle and won. He found that with God he could overcome his problem.

Johnny Cash's experience gives us a real action formula. "Let God go to work on you." He will work you over until you can handle any problem no matter how tough it may be. Think God. Think God. Think God. And then let Him do the work in you. He will.

Still another procedure is to believe in God in depth and

to nourish that belief until you learn to trust. Belief is intellectually based. It involves acceptance of the truth of God in one's thinking. Trust may be defined as belief activated. In this instance you rest completely and wholly on your faith, trusting it to sustain you and see you through whatever, wherever, and whenever the crisis. When you feel inadequate to meet and deal with a problem that seems overwhelming, the practice of trust in God brings to your aid immense and unsuspected resources.

ACTION FORMULA

1. Get God's telephone number (Jer 33:3).
2. Practice the presence of God.
3. Work on developing your capacity to believe.
4. Believe your way out of a mental overcast. Faith dissipates gloominess.
5. Objectify the Divine Presence. Practice His reality.
6. Believe and affirm that, since God is for you, nothing can be against you.
7. Make use of the powerful God thought.
8. Practice trust until you can trust. Then trust.

STEP NUMBER SIX

Prayer Can Overcome

To HANDLE any problem successfully, pray your way over it. This is the surest and safest way to overcome any problem. And it is safe and sure, for it draws upon insight and wisdom that is bound to be superior to your own, involving as it does the guidance of the greatest mind of all.

Utilize the think-pray formula. Human intelligence plus Divine intelligence is more than sufficient to handle successfully any problem you will ever be called upon to face in life. What you can't think of, God can. The answers that you do not know, He does.

A procedure which many have found effective is to sit down and carefully write out your problem in detail. You will know more certainly exactly what you have to deal with. And more than likely as you write it out you will at once begin to see new lines of approach hitherto obscured. As a result there will begin to come to you the happy feeling that you can, after all, overcome this problem.

Seeing it more definitively, you can now proceed to make it come out as it should. Writing makes for organization, for unraveling and clarification. Reduce the problem to its simplest one, two, threes and then the steps leading to solution will start falling in place. By harmonizing your thinking with that of the Lord you can have within you that mind "which was also in Christ Jesus" (Philippians 2:5). How can you go wrong when Jesus Christ is thinking along with you? He knows the score in every instance. His guidance can be yours.

Having written the problem out in the detailed manner described, the next step in the process of solution is to attack the situation with prayer. And that prayer must of course be more than a kind of frantic, "God help me!" appeal. Indeed, if the frantic element is involved it can frustrate the cool rational thinking by which anything is thought through. The secret is to employ prayer in depth, and this kind of prayer requires discipline and sustained effort.

Let me tell you about a young man who became literally a genius in getting right solutions to problems.

From a floundering person, defeated most of the time, he developed into an extraordinarily competent individual. To his problems he got answers that really answered. The method he evolved was amazing in the high score he attained in right solutions.

His method consisted, first, of writing the problem in meticulous detail. Then he studied what he had written, and in instances where he lacked familiarity with some particular factor he would assiduously research it. "You can't think in the dark. You've got to know all you can about everything involved," he explained. "Otherwise you may miss the point of the whole thing."

Having done his own mental homework, he was now ready "to get a real mind going" for him, to use his own words. "I had evolved my own ideas by now, as to the steps to take and the decisions to make. But since I'm a human being I can think wrong, very wrong, and make stupid choices. Therefore, I now set about getting the Lord's ideas and decisions." This he did by first reading favorite sections in the Bible, reminding himself of such explicit promises as "Thou shalt guide me with thy counsel" (Psalm 73:24). This conditioned the mind to be receptive to God's suggestions and got him into spiritual harmony so that the guidance insights could come through.

He would then "tell the Lord" of his own desires, the kind of answers he would like and the solution as it appeared to him. But then he would add, "But if what I want isn't good and if my solutions are off the beam, please make me willing to accept, instead, what You want for me. And please brief me on Your decisions. I want to do it Your way."

Following this mental and spiritual conditioning, the young man then practiced what he called a "quiet time," body relaxed, mind unhurried and peaceful. The agitated and ruffled-up mind can often prevent insights from arising out of the deeper levels of consciousness. Accordingly, it is of the utmost importance to cultivate, by meditation, a relaxed, quiescent state to open up lines of spiritual communication.

Now I want to re-stress something mentioned in an earlier section, though differently applied. It is the positive-thinking-prayer approach to a problem. Add to this the sincere effort to do all that you possibly can about a problem situation. Then, as St. Paul so wisely said, "Having done all . . . stand" (Ephesians 6:13). Let go and let God. It will then work out as it should, which means as He wants it to be.

But for our human part of the action a further ingredient is required. That ingredient is persistence. Never give up. Keep going, whatever the adversities. Face the problem calmly and intelligently. Examine the circumstances and do everything you can think to do about it. And never give up either in your thoughts or in your actions. Pray and believe and bring positive thinking to bear upon the situation. *And never give up.*

When everything seems to be going wrong, you have a great opportunity for practicing the positive mental prayer attitude, believing that with God's help you can achieve your objective. If you think something is hopeless, your state of mind will actually attract further trouble to defeat you. Hold the thought that conditions will shift in your favor—and get going.

The glib idea of "circumstances beyond our control" is too often used to rationalize a feeble giving up too soon. "I don't believe in circumstances," said George Bernard Shaw. "The people who get on in this world are the people who get up and look for the circumstances they want, and, if they can't find them, make them." That is the attitude that works wonders in problems.

ACTION FORMULA

1. Pray your way over your problem—pray confidently.
2. Utilize the think-pray formula.
3. Write out your problem in detail to externalize the problem, rather than allow it to bog down in your mind.
4. Be sure to reduce the human error element by emphasizing God's truth.
5. Practice the quiet time to get the mind quiescent, thus allowing intuitions from deeper levels to float to the surface.
6. Do all that you can, then leave the results to God. Let go and let God.
7. Practice mental and spiritual thought conditioning.
8. Never give up, never—always keep going for right solutions.

STEP NUMBER SEVEN

There Is a Solution to Every Problem

NEVER will you have a problem so great that it cannot be overcome. Just keep that fact in mind; it is a basic truth. Of course, this is not to say that you will have only easy problems. Indeed, you may have some that are incredibly difficult, great big problems that may seem completely overwhelming. But by your ability to think and pray and endure and strive and believe—you can overcome any problem life brings.

Never say that anything is hopeless. As someone once

pointed out, "There are no hopeless situations, only hopeless people." Under no circumstances let yourself become so discouraged and negative as to give in to the feeling that you cannot see your way through a problem. Never, never, never give up, as Churchill once advised. Only those who give up are defeated by problems. The Lord has made this world so that man has the capacity to meet and think through and pray through any problem no matter how tough or complex it may be. Man has been given inner powers over his problems. As the Scripture puts it, "I have the strength to face all conditions by the power that Christ gives me" (Philippians 4:13, *Good News for Modern Man*).

One of the powers given you is that of being able to "hear," by the deep inward ear which connects with your basic consciousness, the voice of God guiding you. Get attuned by thought and prayer and profound meditation and you can draw so near to God that His guidance will definitely come through. And especially is this true in crisis when suddenly great need is thrust upon you for the handling of which you feel totally incompetent. It is then that you will discover that all the time you have possessed an inner capacity that draws greater power to your aid.

For example, consider the story of Beth Black as she wrote it for *Guideposts* Magazine. One clear, star-studded night Mrs. Black was the sole passenger in a small plane piloted by her husband. They were over Dallas, Texas and enjoyed the lights strung like necklaces over the terrain below.

Suddenly Mr. Black gasped and slumped dead in his seat of a heart attack. Frozen with grief and terror, Mrs. Black was desperate. At first she thought of letting the plane crash so that she could die with her husband. But the thought of their young children at home deterred her.

She knew nothing at all about flying except that if you turned the wheel right or left the plane would bank in those directions and if you pushed the wheel forward the plane would nose down. If you pulled it back the aircraft would rise. But she was beside herself with panic. The gauges on the instrument panel were an incomprehensible jumble. She knew if she were to have any chance at all to survive she would have to get through to the control tower to receive guidance. She picked up the radio microphone. Frantically she cried into the various frequencies, "Help! Someone! Oh, God, please help me!" It was a desperate and urgent prayer.

And the prayer was being answered. Even this desperate problem was proving possible to overcome. For amidst the static came a clear voice from the airport tower. Finally the voice got through her fears, guiding her step by step to an incredible but safe landing. This woman, who had never flown a plane, who had watched aghast as her husband died, found astonishingly that she possessed an inner power hitherto unrealized.

Who can say that behind the human voice in the control tower is not a greater Voice in a bigger control tower guiding all who trust to a solution to every problem? Flying blind in life as we often do, we can still listen for that Voice. It will release power in you. Then you will know that every problem has its solution to which you will be guided.

Mr. W. Clement Stone, whom I have often cited, has a fantastic attitude toward problems. I telephoned him at his Chicago office relative to a matter in which we were both interested. "We have a problem," I declared.

"That's wonderful!" he shouted back. "That's good, a problem is always good. It means we may find better ways of doing things. And always remember, to every disadvantage there is an advantage." Mr. Stone, who has spent his entire life taking problems apart, believes without question that every problem has its solution and that anyone can find it who really believes that he can.

Another friend, Stanley Arnold, came up with a phrase that deserves to be a classic. "Every problem contains the seeds of its own solution." The secret of problem solving is to look for those seeds, some of which may be very small, but can lead to the center of the problem itself. Work with what you know about a problem, follow each factor back to its connection with the main matter at issue.

A businessman consulted me. He was very discouraged about a problem connected with his company. Having been for some days unable to find an answer, he was now on the verge of panic, so much so that his mind had frozen and was no longer operative. Certainly it was not delivering the necessary ideas.

He outlined the problem in detail. I encouraged him to talk and gave him plenty of time, in the hope that he might, as sometimes is the case, talk himself into a solution. But it did not work that way. Indeed, the more he talked and wrestled with the problem the more his tension increased, effectively closing off any possible creative thought. "There just is no solution to this one," he said dejectedly. "I'm completely licked."

"Oh, no, you are not," I replied. "And there is a solution to this problem. I'm sure of that because I've never yet seen a problem without a solution. Problems and solutions inevitably go together. You cannot have one without the other being right there all the time."

I then suggested the mental defusing method by which the tension is broken by turning away from the problem.

"Let's forget it for a little while," I suggested. "Set it aside and for ten minutes or so let us think about God instead."

The man asked how you thought about God. And we discussed this totally different type of thought for a few minutes. All of this served to start a mental reconditioning and quieting of the mind. Then, stopping the discussion, I said, "We will sit here quietly and think about God and Jesus Christ." I instructed my secretary not to interrupt us and for at least ten minutes the two of us sent our thoughts Godward. I knew it was being effective, for the atmosphere seemed actually to deepen, taking on an unmistakable spiritual sensitivity.

Finally he broke the silence. "This is the first time I have felt relaxed and peaceful in days. I actually feel—" he searched for a word "—refreshed. That's it! I feel refreshed. I'm really untensed. What did you call it—'mental defusing?' Well, it works. I'm defused."

He arose to leave. "Thanks a lot," he said. At the door he turned. "What do you know? That's funny," he mused, more to himself than to me. "Why, that's it. Of course it is. Why haven't I thought of it before?"

"Meaning what?" I asked.

"Meaning that I've got the beginning of the solution of my problem. You're right. You're so right," he said. "Indeed there is a solution to every problem." Bypassing the problem through spiritual meditation defused him and permitted the solution to float to the surface of his mind. He discovered you can overcome any problem. So keep on believing, thinking, praying.

ACTION FORMULA

1. Believe there is a solution to every problem. Erase all doubts.

2. Never give up trying for the solution. Any problem will yield ultimately to sustained effort.

3. Affirm your capacity to solve your problem.

4. Cultivate the power to "hear" by the inward ear and thus receive God's guidance.

5. Remind yourself that every disadvantage has a corresponding advantage.

6. Never forget that every problem contains the seeds of its own solution.

7. Practice meditation and experience mental defusing.

8. Keep on believing, thinking, praying.

PART FOUR:

What to Do When

INTRODUCTION

How to Let Spiritual Teachings Help You

THE PURPOSE of this section is to help you when you need help the most.

Many people have said, "Problems seem to pounce upon me suddenly when I am not ready to handle them. What do I do when that happens?"

Any spiritual student of life knows that troubles are a part of human experience and that God will help us ready ourselves to successfully deal with the vicissitudes of human existence.

The wise person, realistically anticipating that troubles will come, accumulates strength in advance. But, not always are we provident enough to have done this. Thus it is that we must get instant help at the time difficulty comes. The following material provides for either method.

Under each trouble heading in the following pages are listed carefully selected Scripture passages, together with comments on the meaning and applicability of these verses. Biblical quotations are from the Revised Standard Version of the Bible. The suggested method for using this material is, first, to read this section in its entirety. Then study each section as your need may dictate. We suggest further that for best results each section be fully mastered by meditation, then by committing the suggested passages to memory. As the verses are allowed to sink into your mind, the sacred words of Scripture will actually modify and change your reactions so that you may master troublesome situations.

These Scripture passages are actually alive in their

working effect. By dwelling upon them, and living by them, you make ready for whatever comes when it comes. You will know WHAT TO DO WHEN.

2/27/06

Hi Beth—

I had Armand find a
copy of this book last Aug.
on Amazon.com. I have had
my own copy since I was
25. Sometimes I use it a lot
& sometimes not so often.
We all miss your Dennis
a lot & think of you often.
I had this really profound letter
to send you [in my mind] only.
I would have had this book
another 10 years if I had
waited to write the "perfect"
letter.
     You & your family are
always in our thoughts
   & prayers.
               Love, Susan
          & everyone else.

WHAT TO DO WHEN

Angry

IT IS very important what you do when angry. On your action rides, to a large extent, the destiny of your life. You can stir up trouble, make enemies, ruin chances, or make yourself sick. On the contrary, by proper handling of anger you can keep situations under control, cement friendships, win respect and stay healthy. I suspect that many people's lives have been ruined by anger. By the same token, the skillful mastering of anger has added to the effectiveness of many.

When angry, the following verses constitute an extraordinarily effective anti-anger technique.

1.

*Good sense makes a man slow to
     anger,
     and it is his glory to over-
     look an offense.*

Proverbs 19:11

This verse pits good sense against anger and stresses the value of imperturbably overlooking offense. When anger surges upon you, just say to yourself, "It is stupid to get mad. It won't get me anywhere except into trouble. The momentary satisfaction of letting go isn't worth the difficulties I will experience as a result." In this manner, you may talk yourself into being sensible. This rational procedure will slow down your anger reactions and help you rise above the provocation. In other words, meet anger with urbanity.

2.

*Know this, my beloved brethren. Let
every man be quick to hear, slow to
speak, slow to anger...*

James 1:19

This verse teaches us to be alert to people and situations, but always to react slowly to emotional stimulae. The longer you can keep quiet, the more effective will be your reactions. Don't say the sharp words, do not make the quick retort, do not write that nasty letter; or, if you do, tear it up. Say nothing. Keep quiet. Make no rejoinder. Practice the great strategy of delay.

3.

*—do not let the sun go down on
your anger.*

Ephesians 4:26

Never let a day end without getting rid of your anger. This advice is psychologically very sound. Empty anger out every night to keep it from accumulating. In your prayers, drain off any anger content that may be in your mind. Forgive everybody and practice the great art of forgetting.

You can build up resistance to anger by letting these verses soak into your thought processes until they exert an automatic check upon your emotional reactions.

WHAT TO DO WHEN
Anxious

OF ALL the thousands of letters I have received, the

problem of worry is most frequently presented. The following have helped many to gain victory over worries.

1.

Hence we can confidently say,
"The Lord is my helper,
I will not be afraid;
what can man do to me?

Hebrews 13:6

Nobody can really hurt you. We do not stand alone in
this world, for we can turn to God and He will actually
help us. Fill your mind with thoughts of God; get in
harmony with God's will; eliminate from your heart all
feelings contrary to love; practice simple trust. God then
can help you. Practice thinking less about your worries
and more about God. Instead of thinking how difficult
your problem is, think how great and powerful God is.
This changes your psychology; but more than that, it
releases spiritual power into your mind. That will enable
you to meet your situation. Always repeat this text when
you are afraid.

2.

Have no anxiety about anything, but in
everything by prayer and supplication
with thanksgiving let your requests be
made known to God.

Philippians 4:6

The method outlined in this verse for casting out anxiety
is fourfold: prayer, supplication, thanksgiving and just
telling God what you want. When you are worried, stop
thinking and talking in an anxious manner, and pray. Ask

God to relieve you of your fears or show you how to handle the problem that causes the fear. Then, immediately upon asking Him, give thanks, thus expressing your belief that He is answering your prayer.

3.

If you sit down, you will not be afraid;
when you lie down, your sleep will
be sweet.

Proverbs 3:24

It is important when dealing with worry to go to sleep at night in the right manner. If you retire with a mind filled with fear thoughts, you will have only superficial sleep for, beneath the surface, anxieties are disturbing you in the deep subconscious. Therefore, when you lie down to sleep, think of God as being with you and watching over you. Place the cares of the day in His hands. Every night say this verse over to yourself before you go to sleep. Then, instead of fears in your subconscious, faith in God's presence will develop a confident approach to life.

WHAT TO DO WHEN
Criticized

AND YOU will be criticized if there is any force whatsoever to your personality. There is just one way to avoid criticism: never do anything, never amount to anything. Get your head above the crowd and the jealous will notice and attack you. Therefore, welcome criticism as a sign that your life has vitality.

Actually, your critic is an asset, though at times an

unpleasant one, for he keeps you alert and causes you to study yourself. These verses may be effectively used when criticized.

1.

Bless those who persecute you; bless and do not curse them.

Romans 12:14

This wise, though admittedly difficult, advice will really work in dealing with criticism. When anybody criticizes you, instead of criticizing him in return, or fighting back at him, or saying unkind things about him, simply bless him. This means, ask God to help him. Pray for his well-being and that his life may be filled with blessings. By following this procedure, your critic, instead of receiving opposition from you, which is destructive, will receive good will, which is creative. You may not win him over by blessing him, but you will remove the sting from yourself and possibly help him overcome his hatefulness.

2.

Repay no one evil for evil, but take thought for what is noble in the sight of all.

Romans 12:17

There is always a tendency, when criticized, to repay in the same coin. Something evil has been done to you and the old Adam in us all wants to give evil in return. But that only makes the whole situation more evil. And it is a simple fact that no good ever comes out of evil.

So, the verse tells us to do that which is noble. When you act small, it is bound to react unfavorably to yourself. But,

when you do the noble thing, the big, generous and right
thing, criticism of you will fail in its intended purpose
because everybody will see that you are big and therefore
the criticism is unwarranted.

3.

*Beloved, never avenge yourselves, but leave
it to the wrath of God; for it is written,
"Vengeance is mine, I will repay, says the
Lord."*

Romans 12:19

It is not our business to get revenge. That is the
prerogative of God. It is He who repays people for wrong
they have done, not you. He does not allow us to exercise
vengeance and thus set ourselves up as judges and punish-
ers. He, alone, is the judge of men's actions. He punishes
where necessary. So, leave it to Him, for He can do it
better than we can, and besides, He does it constructively.

Never answer back, never explain, keep your spirit
right. Learn all you can from your critic, honestly analyze
and correct yourself where necessary. Then, go on doing
your job to the best of your ability.

WHAT TO DO WHEN
Disappointed

WHEN YOU are in the gloom of disappointment, sound,
straight thinking is called for. Disappointment can cause
you to be so emotionally disturbed and depressed that you
will be unable to think effectively. As a result, you cut off

the creative forces that are ready to help you the minute
you become helpable.

Disappointment is a prevailing and common adversary
of the human spirit and may strike you at most any time.
Therefore, one should learn to deal with it. Four verses can
be of great help.

1.

Therefore, do not throw away your
confidence, which has a great reward.

Hebrews 10:35

When disappointment strikes, simply hold tight to your
confidence. Do not petulantly throw it away. Affirm, "I am
still confident. I still believe." It will require some mental
and spiritual effort to maintain confidence. Your tendency
may be, in a kind of desperation, to throw it away. So,
focus your mind by an act of will on confidence. The
promise of the text is that such practice will bring great
reward.

2.

Bless the Lord, O my soul,
and forget not all his benefits.

Psalm 103:2

The practice of thanksgiving is a great viewpoint
changer. This verse, subtle in wisdom, tells you to start
thanking the Lord for all the benefits He has given you,
instead of mentally, and perhaps vocally, harping on what
has been denied you.

3.

—be content with what you have;
for he has said, "I will never fail
you nor forsake you."

Hebrews 13:5

The word contentment derives from two Latin words, con and tenere, meaning to hold together. When you have faith in God, your mind will hold together so efficiently that you can recover from disappointment. Thus, you can be content, and out of such contentment great things can happen.

4.

We know that in everything God works
for good with those who love him, who
are called according to his purpose.

Romans 8:28

When disappointed, just practice loving God all the harder. Carefully analyze yourself to make certain you are thinking and living in harmony with His spiritual purpose. It could be that you are off the spiritual beam. Instead of dwelling upon the word "disappointment," think of it as "His-appointment." What you regard as a disappointment may actually be a wonderful new appointment or plan for your life; namely, His plan.

It is wise, always, to take a positive view toward disappointment. It could be that through disappointment you are being shown another way or being led toward something different. If you have tried sincerely and prayerfully and things have not gone well, then look upon disappointment as an opportunity to ask whether you should go, under God's guidance, in another direction.

WHAT TO DO WHEN
Discouraged

ALL HUMAN beings are subject to elevated and depressed moods because of the rhythmic element in all life. Human nature has its time of the upbeat and its time of the downbeat. The problem isn't whether or not discouragement will come, for it will. The question is, have you the spirit and skill to meet it efficiently? That skill may be developed by using the following verses.

1.

Wait for the Lord; be strong,
*   and let your heart take courage;*
*   yea, wait for the Lord!*

Psalm 27:14

The technique suggested of waiting for the Lord is to condition your mind to think about God rather than your difficulties. As you dwell on your troubles they tend to grow large and become dominating. By this distorted thinking you build them up. But, as you concentrate your thoughts upon God, your difficulties will shrink to actual size. This healthy and rational thinking then enables you to handle troubles effectively.

2.

The Lord is good, a stronghold
*   in the day of trouble;*
*   he knows those who take refuge*
*   in him.*

Nahum 1:7

Here is suggested something great to think about when black discouragement clouds your mind; simply, that the Lord is good. Everything cannot have gone bad, for the Lord is good. Think of the Lord as a stronghold from which you may come forth with spiritual reinforcements to confront your difficulties with new power. He knows your troubles and will stand by you.

3.

Why are you cast down, O my soul, and
why are you disquieted within me?
Hope in God; for I shall again praise
him, my help and my God.

Psalm 42:11

The cure for depression is hope. But it is more than vague hope. It is hope in God. Practice the belief that God will drive off discouragement. The enormous relief experienced will make you want to praise Him. Let the bright star of hope in God shine in your mind in the dark night of discouragement.

The power of these three passages is very great. They can be like a shaft of sunlight through the darkness if you saturate your consciousness with them. To do that, say them aloud over and over again in every time of discouragement.

WHAT TO DO WHEN

Frustrated

A NEUROLOGIST says that many nervous breakdowns may be traced to long-held and persistent frustration. "Why do things go so badly with me?" "Why do so many difficulties get in my way?" "Why, all of a sudden, does one thing after another go wrong?" These are the complaints that we hear and which lie at the bottom of that state of petulance, irritation and exasperation which we call frustration. For the healing of this condition, the following passages are helpful.

1.

Many are the afflictions of the right-
eous;
but the Lord delivers him out of
them all.

Psalm 34:19

This text recognizes that there are afflictions that may be suffered even by those who are attempting to live right. But we are told that the Lord will deliver us out of all such trouble. Our part is simply to put frustration in the hands of the Lord. Then, having left it with Him, we must go ahead and do our best, knowing that He will bring things to a state of rightness so that the perverseness which frustrated us will no longer prevail.

So, when frustrated, deliberately practice thinking as calmly as possible and continue doing things the best you know how. In addition, reaffirm your faith in the Lord, knowing that in due time He will deliver you out of your frustration.

2.

"Agree with God, and be at peace;
thereby good will come to you."

Job 22:21

This is a very subtle passage for dealing with frustration. It tells us to agree with God, to get in harmony with Him. Frustrations may arise from the fact that we are trying to insist upon our own way. And it could indicate that we are not going at things correctly, since resistance is encountered. I do not mean to indicate that we are right only when there is no resistance. But when everything seemingly gets in the way and continues to do so, and doors are persistently shut, it may indicate that we ought to re-think our objectives and goals. It suggests a reappraisal of method. Are we working at the right thing or going at it the right way?

So, when frustrated, pray and think your problem through, always asking the question: "Am I in harmony with God?" In other words, am I agreeing with God? When you are, then things will go better.

3.

Commit your way to the Lord;
trust in him, and he will act.

Psalm 37:5

Prayerfully decide what you want to accomplish. Then, put the matter in the hands of God, asking guidance and help. Believe He is with you. Put your whole trust in the fact that He is.

I like the way in which the text ends, "and he will act." That is to say, God will not encourage us without giving assistance. You can expect results if you commit your way to the Lord, trust Him, work hard, and do your part. You can have confidence that God will act and things will come out right, no matter how many difficulties may have frustrated you.

WHAT TO DO WHEN

Ill

IT IS generally recognized today that a direct relationship exists between spiritual and emotional attitudes and health. So many people are ill as a result of wrong thinking. Psychosomatic illness (that is, the effect of unhealthy mental states upon the body) has developed so extensively that a new emphasis is needed upon religion as a healing therapy. Therefore, when illness comes, the following verses are designed to have a healthful application.

1.

And he went about all Galilee...
healing every disease and every in-
firmity among the people.

Matthew 4:23

During an illness, the coming of the doctor always brings hope and reassurance. Doctors are able to heal effectively, not only due to their skill and knowledge, but also because the patient has faith in them.

So, in your illness, practice faith in Christ as a Healer. Form a definite mental image of the Master visiting you and laying His hand of healing upon you. Hold in mind the picture which the text presents; that of Jesus going about healing people. Conceive of yourself as among those who experience the healing grace of Christ. Use this affirmation, "The healing grace of Jesus Christ is working in me now."

2.

*"Let not your hearts be troubled;
believe in God, believe also in me."*

John 14:1

This is one of the most comforting passages in the Bible
and it also has healing power. When you keep your heart
from being troubled with anxiety or any other disturbing
factor, your physical being will more completely respond
to the healing ministrations of your physician. Think of
this text as actually applying to your physical heart and
affirm, "The healing touch of the Lord is on my physical
heart and He who created my body is now helping it to
function normally."

As you repeat this verse, visualize your body, mind and
soul as entering into a state of harmonious well-being.

3.

*—and the prayer of faith will save
the sick man.*

James 5:15

Use prayers of faith in your illness. They will save you
from that despondency which retards recovery. Such
prayers will attune your mind to God and permit His
healing forces to operate in you. These forces are quietness
of mind, creative hope, the joyful experience of the
presence of Christ and the conviction that God's restora-
tive energy is within you. You will discover that the prayer
of faith is one of the most powerful influences in getting
your spirit into that state of adjustment wherein God and
the doctor can more effectively make you well.

WHAT TO DO WHEN

Nervous

PEOPLE everywhere are tense and nervously overwrought. The high tempo of modern life has taken its toll of the many who seem unable to adjust to over-pressurized demands. Following are passages that teach tension control and put a quieting hand upon our nervousness.

1.

And the peace of God, which passes all understanding, will keep your hearts and your minds in Christ Jesus.

Philippians 4:7

An effective treatment for nervousness is to use this verse at frequent intervals. Say it slowly, letting its melody and meaning fall softly into your thoughts. Take plenty of time to contemplate the vast peace of God, which is so deep and full and kindly that we cannot comprehend it. Yet it floods into one's life with such health-giving force that nervousness passes, leaving us calm and in control of ourselves.

It is worth all our effort to achieve, finally, the peace of God in body, mind and soul. When you possess the peace of God, you will have conquered nervousness.

2.

... I will be with you; I will not fail you or forsake you.

Joshua 1:5

When you know that you will never be left alone nor forsaken, your nervousness will give way to confidence.

Nervousness is caused many times by insecurity, by self-doubt, by the awesome feeling that you fight life's battles alone. What peace and courage one may derive from this great verse, for it reassures us that God will stand by to help and support and protect throughout our whole life.

3.

Be still before the Lord, and wait patiently for him;

Psalm 37:7

This verse simply tells you to be still. Of course, that is very difficult for a nervous person to do. But the writer of the Psalms knew that full well. So, his advice is more subtle. He tells us to "be still before the Lord." By that is meant to form a picture in your mind of the greatness, the goodness, the peace of God. Let yourself grow quiet as you reflect upon God's enormous and pervasive quietness. Then, simply wait until you hear Him speak words of refreshment, serenity and quietness to you. Your taut nerves will then relax because your mind, which controls your nerves, is filled with God's quietness.

WHAT TO DO WHEN

Rejected

THE ABILITY to get along with people and to be in good relations with others is most important. Yet, many suffer from isolation, not being one of the group, not really belonging. Such people suffer the psychological pain of rejection. How can one truly be in fellowship with others,

be accepted by them, and become competent in the
ability to get along successfully with people?

1.

*And above all these put on love, which
binds everything together in perfect
harmony.*

Colossians 3:14

The key word in getting along with other people is love.
When you have an outflowing attitude of genuine good
will, it has the effect of binding people to you and creating
a state of harmony between them and yourself. When,
even unconsciously, you send out a contrary spirit, it tends
to separate you from the group, for instinctively people
feel whether you like them or not. So, the first step in
getting along with people is to practice genuine love until
it becomes second nature. Then you will attract others and
not repel them.

2.

*Talk no more so very proudly,
    let not arrogance come from your
        mouth;
for the Lord is a God of knowledge,
    and by him actions are weighed.*

I Samuel 2:3

The key thought here is humility. People naturally turn
from the proud and the arrogant. The psychological fact is
that the shrinking person tends to compensate for his
inferiority feelings by arrogant actions and a proud manner. Thus, while he really isn't that type of person at heart,

yet he seems so. The result is that people do not like him. Therefore, take care that you do not speak or act arrogantly, but cultivate the spiritual virtue of humbleness.

3.

Love one another with brotherly
affection; outdo one another in showing
honor.

Romans 12:10

This passage urges you to like people so genuinely that you can sublimate yourself and be sincerely desirous of putting others ahead of yourself. Observe those who get along best with their fellowmen and you will invariably see that they are always putting the other fellow foremost.

The practice of these three Biblical principles will help you become a harmonious member of the group.

WHAT TO DO WHEN
Resentful

RESENTMENT IS a widespread cause of failure and illness. The person who lives above resentment will have joy, serenity and a wondrous state of well-being. Also, he will have fewer enemies than those who practice retaliation. Here are three verses to help you.

1.

The north wind brings forth rain;
and a backbiting tongue, angry
looks.

Proverbs 25:23

What a graphic picture this verse presents. Even as the north wind drives dark rain clouds before it, so does a mean tongue stir up storms. Black clouds appear on people's faces and mean feelings are generated in their hearts. The light of reason is cast aside. Ill will prevails. Emotional reactions govern relationships.

How different when one does not backbite, but rather, with self-control, maintains composure. Then there are no storms, only peacefulness.

2.

Let all bitterness and wrath and anger
and clamor and slander be put away from
you, with all malice, and be kind to
one another, tenderhearted, forgiving one
another, as God in Christ forgave you.

Ephesians 4:31-32

Here is an explicit blueprint for skillful living. Christians, very definitely, are people who hold no bitterness, who do not become angry or have malice. Those qualities simply do not belong in one who follows Christ. A Christian is a person who is kind, tenderhearted and forgiving. If you allow yourself to be guilty of bitterness, wrath, anger, clamor (gossipy talking) and slander, you will suffer from the malady of resentment which eats away your health and happiness. Better say this text to yourself often so that it may govern your reactions.

3.

... "if your enemy is hungry, feed him;
if he is thirsty, give him drink; for

by so doing you will heap burning coals
upon his head."

Romans 12:20

Instead of allowing yourself to hold resentment, use spiritual strategy; do something for your enemy. This can be accomplished by speaking well of him and in every way being just as nice to him as he has been mean to you. If you fight him back and give him just as good as he sends, the hostility will deepen. But if, on the contrary, you give him good for evil, you will baffle him so that in due time you may actually win him over. The greatest thing to do with an enemy is to make him your friend.

The consistent practice of these verses will siphon off resentment.

WHAT TO DO WHEN

Sorrowful

SORROW GIVES the human heart a profound shock. Probably no human experience cuts so deeply into the very center of one's life as the loss of a loved one. But sorrow is a part of human experience and is one of the inevitables with which we deal. There is no bright or easy philosophy that will shield a person from the necessity of meeting its cold, hard weight at some time in his life. Therefore, we must be prepared to meet it when it comes.

Of course, the book to turn to for a philosophy that will enable you to meet sorrow and find relief is the Holy Bible. It is filled with messages from God that help to alleviate the anguish and pain.

1.

For his anger is but for a moment,
and his favor is for a lifetime.
Weeping may tarry for the night,
but joy comes with the morning.

Psalm 30:5

Your agony is not permanent and what seems to be the cold, stern face of God is only momentary, while His favor, His kindliness and His love are for all your life. Though you may weep and be brokenhearted and a dark night seems to settle down upon you, it will pass. Morning will come and with it understanding and, ultimately, joy. So you can carry on through the darkness of sorrow, for He will bring you to a new day.

2.

He will wipe away every tear from their
eyes, and death shall be no more,
neither shall there be mourning nor
crying nor pain any more, for the former
things have passed away.

Revelation 21:4

This is one of the most beautiful passages ever written. It pictures God as our great, kindly Father comforting his brokenhearted children. Even as our parents took us in their arms when we were young and wiped away our tears, so God, great parent of humanity, comforts us. As we live with Him we will enter into an understanding and depth of life where pain, mourning and crying shall pass away in His Heavenly Kingdom. The ultimate end of human experience is not sadness, but eternal goodness.

3.

As a father pities his children,
so the Lord pities those who fear him.

Psalm 103:13

I like this text because it describes God as having pity in His heart for His children. His kindliness and sympathy are always ours and in our sorrow He weeps with us. We read that "Jesus wept." Thus Divinity shares human grief.

4.

The Lord is near to the broken-
hearted, and saves the crushed in spirit.

Psalm 34:18

Again, we have the reassurance of God's nearness. When you feel utterly crushed by the tragedy and sorrow of life, say this beautiful verse aloud and feel His kindly presence renewing your depressed spirit.

WHAT TO DO WHEN
Tempted

" 'IT'S NO sin to be tempted,' Peter Marshall used to say. 'It isn't the fact of having temptations that should cause us shame, but what we do with them. Temptation is an opportunity to conquer. When we eventually reach the goal to which we are all striving, God will look us over, not for diplomas, but for scars.' "*

Temptation, in one form or another, attacks each of us.

*A *Man Called Peter* by Catherine Marshall. McGraw-Hill Book Company, New York, NY 10020

But fortunately, we have spiritual weapons for gaining victory over it. One is the following verse.

1.

No temptation has overtaken you that is
not common to man. God is faithful, and
He will not let you be tempted beyond
your strength, but with the temptation
will also provide the way of escape, that
you may be able to endure it.

I Corinthians 10:13

This assures us that no temptation will ever come that has not been faced by others. And if others can overcome it, so can you. Moreover, God will not allow any temptation to attack you which you are not able to overcome. That is a very constructive thought to hold in mind. No matter how strong a temptation may be, it is not beyond your strength; you have the inner power to defeat it. God understands the problem of temptation and has given you a way out. These facts—namely that God is faithful, that He will not allow you to be tempted more than you are able to stand, and that, along with the temptation, He provides a way out of it—encourage you to know you can conquer your temptation.

2.

Let the wicked forsake his way,
 and the unrighteous man his thoughts;
let him return to the Lord, that he
 may have mercy on him,

and to our God, for he will abun-
dantly pardon.

Isaiah 55:7

Temptation is in our thoughts. Therefore, to overcome temptation, simply think right until your thoughts are good thoughts and not bad ones. Then you will have the power to stop wrongdoing and return in thought, purpose and dedication to God. When one does this he receives forgiveness and pardon.

3.

"The Spirit of the Lord is upon
*   me,*
because he has anointed me to
*   preach good news to the poor.*
He has sent me to proclaim release to
*   the captives*
and recovering of sight to the blind,
to set at liberty those who are
*   oppressed. . ."*

Luke 4:18

People who are the victims of recurring temptation through their weakness are indeed "captives." They fully understand what Charles Dickens had in mind when he said. "I wear the chains forged in life." The worst prisons are not made of iron bars and stone, but of thoughts. We imprison ourselves by our sins. But when we repent and surrender ourselves to Christ and want freedom from our sins, He sets us free.

WHAT TO DO WHEN
Tired

THE BURDENS and responsibilities of life sometimes rest heavily upon us and our strength seems insufficient. Many demands make us weary and tired and it is not good to be tired, unless fatigue is balanced by a normal renewal of strength.

The following verses may be helpful when tired.

1.

... I will strengthen the weak ...

Ezekiel 34:16

Those five glorious words mean, simply, that when weak, God will strengthen you. Did you ever stop to consider where you get your energy? It is from God. When that energy runs down and you feel weak and tired you can go back to Him, and He who created your energy can recreate it. Turn to God asking for increased vitality, and you will receive it. Remember those other words, "In Him was life." He will give life to you if you ask it of Him and live according to His will. Thus, you can overcome weakness and abnormal tiredness will no longer be a problem.

2.

... let us also lay aside every
weight, and sin which clings so closely,
and let us run with perseverance the
race that is set before us, looking to
Jesus the pioneer and perfecter of our faith ...

Hebrews 12:1, 2

One way to overcome tiredness is to lay aside the heavy weights that sap your strength; such weights as fear, hate, irritation and all types of sin. In fact, the latter is the heaviest of all weights and is specifically mentioned in the verse. And little wonder, for sin puts an abnormal burden on the mind and it becomes very heavy. In time sin becomes an intolerably heavy weight, so it must be laid aside if we are to run the race of life and win. Go ahead with perseverance, keeping Jesus in mind. He will sustain you always.

By the practice of faith no person need be the victim of abnormal tiredness. Through average rest you can be renewed with vitality every day.

3.
... "My presence will go with you,
and I will give you rest."

Exodus 33:14

We treat ourselves very badly by driving ourselves into a state of exhaustion, straining and pushing and tugging under life's heavy weights and responsibilities. We live as though there was no unhurried flow of power available to us. Tragically enough, many have seemingly forgotten how to rest and renew their energy. Simply become very aware of God's presence, realizing that He will help you with your responsibilities. He will show you how to work with conservation of energy, how to work in a relaxed manner and feel rested, rather than tired. To get yourself into this mood and manner of living, frequently say this verse and meditate upon it.

WHAT TO DO WHEN
Unhappy

MANY PEOPLE are vaguely unhappy. But one should awaken every morning with a thrill in the heart, looking forward with eager anticipation to the day. We should have the time of our lives all day long and actually regret to go to bed for fear of missing something.

Three verses will help cast off unhappiness and show how to live joyfully.

1.

This is the day which the Lord has
made;
let us rejoice and be glad in it.

Psalm 118:24

This is a stimulating tonic with which to begin the day. Upon awakening, say these dynamic words aloud. God has given you a new day crammed with opportunity to build a better life, to add to your knowledge, to have fellowship with those you love, to do something worthwhile for the world. As you go to work, repeat the verse and, if you begin to run down in spirit during the day, say it again. This is one of the greatest of all vitality-producing thoughts. Possibly no method is more effective in driving off unhappiness than to saturate the mind and soul with this great passage.

2.

Rejoice in the Lord always; again I
will say, Rejoice.

Philippians 4:4

We make ourselves unhappy by habitually thinking unhappy thoughts. The cure is to start thinking joyfully. It is that simple. Practice rejoicing, not vaguely, but specifically rejoicing in the Lord. Think of every wonderful thing the Lord has done for you, most important of which is that He is always with you. When you consider the implications of that fact, there is every reason to rejoice and be happy, for it means that nothing can ever defeat you.

3.

Blessed are the people who know
*   the festal shout,*
who walk, O Lord, in the light of
*   thy countenance,*
who exult in thy name all the day,
*   and extol thy righteousness.*

Psalm 89:15-16

Real and dedicated Christians are happy people. That does not mean that they are unaware of the pain and suffering of human existence. Indeed, they are deeply concerned people. They are not true Christians unless they are doing something about it, too. But also, they are filled with joyous exultation, for have they not entered into that priceless experience of Christ which gives victory over all misery?

What a graphic picture—"People who know the festal shout . . . exult . . . all the day long." To be happy, be truly Christian in experience, faith and service.

PART FIVE:

The Power To Change Your Life

INTRODUCTION:

You Can Change Your Life

MOST OF US will admit that some things need changing in our lives. Discordant elements in personality often contribute to failure and unhappiness. We may possess traits which turn people off and interfere with good personal relationships. Perhaps certain weaknesses and inadequacies plague us. Things may seem to go wrong much of the time. Under such circumstances you will welcome the good news that there is available the power to change your life.

And that is what this section, "The Power to Change Your Life," is about. People in great numbers write us at our Foundation for Christian Living about all sorts of problems: difficulties in marriage, family conflict, financial worries, job concerns, young people in trouble, all kinds of matters that bear on the difference between a happy, successful life and an existence full of frustration, conflict and disaster.

We'd be glad to hear from you, and if you are not already receiving our monthly publication, *Creative Help for Daily Living,* we would be pleased to send it to you regularly. Simply write to the Foundation for Christian Living, Pawling, N.Y. 12564.

I believe every individual possesses the inherent ability to conduct his life in an orderly and satisfying manner. He can control and correct any deficiencies or problems in personality that are presently hampering effectiveness. Anyone can become a happy person when and if he really wants to be just that. It is our belief that the person who now "rubs people the wrong way" can learn and master the art of genuinely pleasant personal relations. Moreover, it is our conviction that a job situation which seems annoying, apparently leading only to a dead end, can be made to be exciting and packed full of opportunity. The family unit can be developed into one of great joy and meaning. Relationships between young people and parents can grow into mutual trust and respect, compatible and harmonious. In fact, there is a formula which, when faithfully and intelligently applied, can bring about such creative improvements that it literally constitutes an exciting new life style.

In this part are suggested definite methods and procedures which have been used successfully in the lives of thousands. They have produced the most remarkable changes. They show in a practical manner how you can have the power to change your life.

This section is also designed as an action manual. Its primary purpose is to help you change your life in such a way that you will find real happiness and peace of mind. It is intended as a guide to truly successful living. Therefore, the element of practice is important. In connection with each section a practice schedule is presented outlining definite steps toward life and situation changing.

The great and wonderful changes that you desire will not come easily. A mere cursory reading of these words will work no magical change in your life. But the consistent, constant practice of the principles set forth will certainly do that. Remember that practice is vital and will result in creative improvement.

May we suggest that you first read and study the passages which seem most directly to deal with your most pressing problem. Prayerfully and with open mind, having a desire to capture the power that can change your life, read that section; then re-read and meditate upon its meanings and affirmations. Then, having accepted its premises, begin with a positive-thinking attitude and sincere faith to practice the action principles outlined.

Practice today and tomorrow and the next day, for at least one week. Do this before going on to another section. Epictetus said, "Repetition is the most classical of all studies." Old habit tracks and old thought patterns may not give way easily. But persistence and repetition will break them down.

If you really want the power to change your life, you can have it. Believe it, practice it, pray for it, and God will reward you with better, happier, more meaningful life than you have hitherto experienced.

I. *What Is the Power to Change Your Life?*

THIS AMAZING power is the life of God in you. It is a vast force which, when focused, produces spectacular changes in personality.

"The Kingdom of God is within you." That is to say, in you are values which can be activated by God's creative spirit. The person, therefore, who feels weak and ineffective, defeated, sinful, has within himself a stored-up force that can effect enormous change. But he cannot do it on his own. He must have the releasing action that comes through the simple act of giving his life to God.

When this self-giving is done with real sincerity, the spiritual power activator takes over. The individual becomes a new person as he experiences the power that can change his life.

An example is a man who drove into my farm home in the country. He was accompanied by his wife. They were gifted people, non-church going. He was a publisher, she a writer—both extraordinarily capable. He said, "Helen and I are unhappy and frustrated. Neither of us is really well physically. Life has gone stale. Actually, we've hit a dead end. We need help." He went on to explain that each to a degree had lost the creative touch. They just didn't seem to have it anymore. And then he added, "We do not want to remain as we are. We want this change you are always talking about. How do we get it?"

Knowing them to be what you might call sophisticated people, I wondered whether they could accept the basic simplicity of contacting the power they were asking for.

So I said, "You are dissatisfied with yourselves as you are, is that correct? Just how dissatisfied are you?"

"Completely," they replied.

"And do I understand that you want to be changed and changed now?" The answer was affirmative.

Then I asked, "Are you willing now to separate from your life everything contrary to the spirit of Christ? And I mean everything!"

After some discussion as to what this entailed, it was evident that they were so desirous of the power to change their lives that they would go the whole distance.

We then went into a process of spiritual catharsis, which involved an honest emptying out of wrong attitudes, such as resentments, hostilities and other mental festers. It was obvious that they meant business. They weren't fooling.

"Now," I continued, "no human being can give you the power to change your life. Only Christ can do that. Therefore, are you now willing to commit yourselves to Christ, accepting Him as your Savior and the renewer of life?"

Each offered a humble and obviously sincere prayer of self-commitment. Always when awareness of need joins with complete sincerity the power is given. They wanted it, they asked for it, they received it.

The change in them over succeeding months was re-markable. Life took on new meaning, deeper joy, greater satisfaction.

They came back the next spring seeming vital and in perfect health. They were excited about everything. Helen was almost ecstatic. "Never have I seen such a spring. The skies are bluer, the sunshine more golden, the songs of the birds are sweeter."

They began applying their talents to inspirational writing. They became active in helping others to find the same wonderful new power they had discovered.

The experience of these people demonstrates the validity of the fundamental and time-tested method for getting the power that changes life, which is:

1. Cultivate the realization that the power to change your life comes through faith in Christ.

2. Try giving yourself and all your problems to God.

3. Practice the relaxed faith principle—"Let go and let God."

4. Ask for the power, want the power, believe you are now given the power. Practice believing that you are now really living on the power.

5. Go through the New Testament making a list of the actual words of Jesus and commit them to memory.

6. Ask yourself what Jesus would do. Then try doing that.

7. Form habits of daily prayer setting specific times and give these prayer periods top priority.

8. Read the New Testament from beginning to end, stopping to study passages which particularly appeal to you.

9. Saturate your consciousness with Christ-centered thoughts.

10. Practice love and good will for people, for the power to change your life responds to love.

II. *You Can Have a Happy Family Life*

A HAPPY family life must start with a happy marriage. And a good marriage has to be made by working at it. It doesn't just happen. My wife Ruth has written a book, *The Adventure of Being a Wife,* in which she points out that a successful marriage is a closely-knit, team relationship between husband and wife. The love, mutual respect and unity existing between them will transmit itself to the other family members. So, to have a happy family life, be sure that the marriage relationship is sound, happy and good.

As Ruth says in her book, "I consider myself one of the most fortunate women alive. Why? Because I am totally married to a man in every sense of the word: physically, emotionally, intellectually, spiritually. We're so close that you couldn't put a knife blade between us. I need him and depend on him completely. He needs and depends on me. We're not two lonely, competing individuals. We're one integrated, mutually responsive, mutually supportive organism—and this is such a marvelous and joyous thing that nothing else in life can even approach it. It's the greatest of all adventures."*

The family unit, husband and wife, children, in-laws, grandparents, has an enormous potential for happiness or unhappiness, for love or for misunderstanding and conflict.

When a family lives together in affection and mutual respect, it results in probably the happiest state of life on

*Quoted by permission from the book *The Adventure of Being a Wife,* by Mrs. Norman Vincent Peale, published by Prentice-Hall, Inc., Englewood Cliffs, N.J. 07632

earth. But when the family is disrupted by misunderstanding and conflict, it creates an unhealthy state, one of continuing adverse effect in the lives of all, especially children.

Even in this era it is not necessary for the generations within a family to be sundered apart by a so-called gap. Parents and children, the older and younger generations of families, need not dwell in mutual mistrust and conflict.

Reasonable, intelligent, sincere human beings of any age can, if they will, live together in peace and, indeed, in joyful relationship. If such a condition does not prevail in your family, this is to remind you that you definitely have the power to change your life within the family.

What steps, then, may be taken to bring about a happy family relationship?

1. All that is necessary to begin the process is for one person within the family, perhaps you, to determine that he or she will begin now to create within himself the upbeat spirit which can rejuvenate the family life. Yes—let it begin with you.

2. Having made that decision, the individual must ask himself or herself this question: "Am I personally contributing to the family happiness or unhappiness?" And be sure you answer that question with absolute honesty.

3. Correct within yourself any mistrust or hostility and practice treating everyone in the family not only with love, but with respect for their opinions. Give them genuine esteem.

4. Consider yourself a love "cell" and act lovingly. Do not tell the family you have decided to be this new way. Just be it. They will pick it up. This new spirit injected by you will have effect. The family in due course will respond accordingly.

Let me tell you about a young man in his late teens, definitely of the "now" generation, rebellious and contemptuous of every generation but his own. His parents got their backs up, the generation gap grew wider, the family drifted apart and the household was in a state of unhappiness.

Then this boy had a deep spiritual experience of Jesus Christ. As a result, he decided that instead of being part of the world's problems he would be part of its cure. Still sticking to his own views but now respecting others' opinions as well, he started practicing love in the family. He became a pleasant and lovable person within himself. Result? ... the family got together on a deeper level. He stimulated change in the others. Indeed, they all changed to a considerable extent. The family became a unit wherein everybody loved and respected each other as people.

5. Every member of the family who is truly interested in family unity will practice holding every other member, young and old, in esteem as persons. If the attitudes and actions of one are not entirely pleasant, still everyone should accept each other as they are and let everyone be himself. Identity of personality must always be respected. On this basis the family will hold together and the basic love within the family will create a climate of good will and—what is equally important—real understanding. This one fact alone will help to change your life in the family.

6. Do not wait for someone else in the family to start changing. And certainly do not expect that everyone is going to change at once, or that change will necessarily come easily. There may be the resistance of long-held resentments, and even prejudice, that will be reduced only by a gradual process. The principal factor is that someone must start the change and let it pick up momentum from there, so that all presently will be involved in a new life within the family.

7. The power to change your life within the family may depend greatly upon a basic Christian spirit. The surest guarantee of family happiness and well-being is to develop a profound faith and reliance upon God for guidance within the home and in all the family connections. When the Bible says, "Except the Lord build the house, they labor in vain that build it" (Psalms 127:1), it is a reminder of a time-tested truth that the family with religious faith tends to overcome problems and meet situations, while families without it often fail.

8. How is this curative, healing Christian spirit generated? One way is to begin a program of definite, earnest prayer for each family member. One person doing this regular type of praying, though he may not mention it to the others, will in time unconsciously motivate others to a new, spiritually-oriented attitude. When prayer becomes a group activity in the family, the members will grow together in a deeper fellowship. It is quite true that the family that prays together stays together.

A 20-year-old girl was considerably upset in trying to find herself. Her attitude had been one of constant hostility, especially toward her father. But one night she had a confrontation with him: "Dad," she said, "you're really nice. In fact, you're a good guy. Tell me what you've been doing. Come on, come clean."

Her father then told her that he had been trying out a program of prayer that he would be able to change his own life and attitudes, be a better father, better husband, better member of the family. He hesitated and then said softly, "I pray for everyone, especially you; for in my heart I guess

I've always had a special feeling for you, despite our conflicts."

"I knew you had been up to something," she said, and for the first time in weeks gave him a kind of love pat. In the following days this father and daughter drew together. And in time their secret leaked out. Ultimately it changed the entire family. They proved the power to change life in the family.

III. *Change Your Life in Your Job*

SINCE MUCH of anybody's life relates to his job, if he wants the power to change his life perhaps he will have to change his job.

There are two ways to change jobs. The obvious one is to leave the job you now have and take another one. But if you do this it is usually assumed that all the things you dislike about the present job will be absent in the new job and that, indeed, everything in the new job will be just fine. And that, of course, isn't necessarily so.

There is a law of human nature that has to be reckoned with: you take yourself wherever you go. You can never get away from yourself. So, when you go from an unhappy job to a new job, you will, in the very nature of the case, take yourself along with you. This means, obviously, that the same weaknesses and wrong attitudes that you had in the old position will, after the first flush of enthusiasm, be there with you the same as ever. So the second way to change jobs is to change yourself. And that can be done within the framework of the present job.

It is also true that many job problems have to do with

adjusting to so-called "difficult" people. Change your attitude toward such people and you change the job situation.

There are many people working at jobs in which there is a much greater potential than they have ever visualized. This is indicated by the fact that a new man will come into a position and find in it values and opportunities that his predecessor never discovered.

You see, the principle of the changed life relates not only to moral change. It also concerns becoming a person with changed attitudes and revitalized personality.

A man consulted me complaining about his job. He said it held no opportunity. It was a dead end. He was going to chuck it and go to something else. I outlined the above concept of dealing with a job. Then I mentioned the name of a dynamic man who was very successful. "What do you think Mr. Smith would do with your present job if he had it?"

He thought a minute and then said, "Well, I'm sure he would make it a success; he always makes everything succeed."

"Yes, but how would he succeed with this job?" I persisted. "What would he do?"

To which he replied, "I just don't know what he would do."

"Well, why not spend a few days trying to think what the highly successful Mr. Smith would do in this job and then you do that."

Later he returned with quite an improved attitude. He said, "The only way I can do what Mr. Smith would do is to become an outgoing person like Mr. Smith is. He is a positive thinker. Guess I'd better start practicing positive thinking, too." Encouraged, he followed his new mental attitude and did a rather creative job on himself. His job performance improved. He got a new job by changing himself in his present job.

Quite often we hear from people who say they cannot get a job because they are "overqualified." That is to say, a company will not employ them because they are too highly educated for the lesser job that is available.

Some few years ago it was a vogue to get an education in engineering. Engineering schools were packed. More engineers were turned out, perhaps, than the present necessity requires. So, there comes a time when it is difficult for the trained engineer to get any job because he is considered overqualified for the jobs available.

Here is how one man got over that hurdle. Highly qualified, he could not find a job suitable to his training. But fortunately he was living on the God's guidance principle. He prayed and God guided him by giving him a practical idea. He was to look around for an industry with which he would like to be associated and apply for a position. This he did, turning in his resumé, which showed engineering degrees. "Sorry, we can't use you. You are overqualified," he was told.

"What jobs are open?" he asked.

One was described in maintenance, but the employing officer said, "You are too qualified for that."

"I think my engineering degrees would help me in that job because I have been taught to think in an orderly fashion. Planning and system are needed no matter what the work is. I will take the job." He said this even though the job would pay him just one-quarter of what he felt he needed.

He studied the maintenance situation in the plant, cut expenses, ordered more efficiently and, as the boss put it, "really had the place ship-shape." His overqualification paid off and he loved the job. Ultimately he became important to the company because of the way he handled this job, which was supposedly beneath him.

He has now moved well up in the firm, still not practicing engineering, but, as he put it, being now in charge of personnel, he is working in "human engineering."

How to change your life in your job:

1. Change the job. See its possibilities. Get excited. Pour enthusiasm into it.

2. Don't keep on saying, "It's a no-good job." Say, "This job is really challenging," and say it no matter what the job is.

3. To change jobs, change yourself. A changed person will have a new view, new attitudes and will put new life into the old job.

4. Do your job the very best you can and with real enthusiasm. That is the best and surest road to promotion.

5. If you are overqualified, take any job you can get and give it all the know-how of your overqualification.

6. Give yourself to your job and it will give itself to you.

IV. *Power When It's Hard Going*

WHEN PROBLEMS and troubles gang up on you, as sometimes they will, the big question is, do you let yourself become overwhelmed, do you feel like giving up?

There will be times when things coming one after another may get you down. But that is of no importance if they don't keep you down.

The big question is your rebound, your comeback

power, your ability to stand up to adversity and handle it creatively. The plain fact is that you or I or anyone who will employ faith in Christ possesses know-how, strength and persistence necessary to meet any situation when it really is hard going. In a word, you have the power to change your life in adversity.

The type of adversity we are referring to consists of such old human problems as not having enough money to stretch over your expenses, unemployment perhaps, or a business expectation that has not worked out, unexpected doctors' bills and hospital expenses, loss of savings, failure in some objective. The list is endless.

There are two possible attitudes to take when things go hard. One is to become discouraged, even hopeless, and to give up, to let go the feeling that you can do something about it. This attitude is, of course, disastrous. For if you admit even to yourself that you do not have the ability to cope with things, your personal resources will not come into action.

The second attitude is to put all of your problems into God's hands and believe positively and optimistically that God and you together can solve the adversity situation. This dynamic faith attitude starts the creative process to functioning.

What are some techniques for handling adversity?

1. Organize an attack on your troubles. You are stronger than all your troubles taken together. But you must organize your mental attack on them. When many things are going wrong, the tendency is to be confused. So first you must bring mental order into the situation.

I once knew a man who labeled himself a "debt doctor." He called on people who were swamped with bills—it seemed to them that they had an overwhelming mass of debt which they just couldn't handle.

To one such debt-burdened family he said, "Let's put all your bills here on the table and add them up. Now let us examine your resources and add them up. The difference is what we have to work with in the reduction of your debts."

Then he examined each bill and said to the harassed couple, "You can pay $1 a week on this account, $2 a week on this one, and 50¢ here."

"But," they objected, "those people would never accept such a small amount. And besides, it can never be paid off at that rate."

But the debt doctor reasoned, "If you tell each account you are going to pay even this small amount regularly and not contract any other indebtedness until it is paid, I believe they will respect you and go along with the arrangement."

They were so relieved to see order out of confusion that they agreed to the program. Not only did they make steady progress in payment, but they became better able to plan and make do and ultimately to get ahead. Instead of being harassed, unhappy, adversity-swamped, they acquired a good measure of control over their lives.

2. *Prayerize* your adversity. That curious word is not original. It was suggested to me by a man who decided to put spiritual techniques into practice in a hard situation he was facing in business. In his prayers he said he received guidance to work out the following three principles: "Prayerize, visualize, actualize." He explained that by this he meant that through prayer he got a clear understanding of how his situation could be improved with God's help. He then practiced visualizing his goal, sharpening that concept until he knew exactly where he wanted to go. He held the image of successful achievement firmly in mind

continuously, visualizing a good outcome. He worked hard toward such realization and finally his prayer guidance and sustained visualization were realized. What he sought became an actual accomplishment.

3. Change your thinking about adversity. Stop thinking adversity and instead think in terms of corrective opportunity. Adopt the philosophy of W. Clement Stone, "To every disadvantage there is a corresponding advantage." No longer think disadvantage. Think advantage. Persist in this process and your mind will begin finally to produce the advantage inherent in the disadvantage. Adopt a positive mental attitude, believing that with God's help you will, out of your own intelligence, create a better state of affairs for yourself and others.

4. Have faith in your ability to think. Do not predicate your situation upon emotional reactions. You can improve your situation by cool, rational thought. Remember, the mind will not function when it is hot, nervous or panicky. Only when it is calm and quiet will it produce those insights which are necessary to the rehabilitation of your circumstances.

5. Get God's thinking working for you. God's is the greatest mind. He understands all about your situation. He knows all the answers necessary to get you out of this trouble and lead you to a substantial state of affairs. And there is a way that you can bring the mind of God into your problem. It is through the prayer and spiritual meditation technique. By this we mean simply to get your mind into a state of quietness. Then start thinking spiritually. To do that, say something like this: "Lord, You know my troubles. I believe that with Your help I can think my way through them. Guide my thinking and give me right answers. Help me do things Your way." As the Scripture

says, "Let this mind be in you, which was also in Christ Jesus" (Philippians 2:5). With the benefit of the Lord's mind you can think straight. You can handle adversity.

No set of adversities can stand up for very long against the individual who draws upon God's thinking.

---

v. *The Power to Get Out of a Rut*

Y EARS AGO in upstate New York I saw a road sign, "Choose Your Rut Well—You'll Be In It for the Next Twenty-five Miles."

The secret of living is to get out of ruts, to set new goals and reach for them.

Marilyn Helleberg wrote a down-to-earth article for *Guideposts* on "How to Aim Yourself,"* outlining practical ways to accomplish more and to reach your goals. Master her technique for "aiming yourself" and you will have the power to change your life.

❝ It was my 35th birthday [she writes] and all day I had been struggling against the gnawing awareness that my life was half over and what did I have to show for a life half-spent? I realized that what I really needed more than anything else was a feeling of achievement. I guess we all need that—almost as much as we need food and water.

As I cleared the table, I thought of how often I had heard myself say, "Gee, I really intended to do that," or "I'd do it if I just had more time," but I never seemed to get anywhere. Maybe my aim was wrong.

The one word, aim, hovered strangely in my thoughts

*Reprinted by permission from *Guideposts* Magazine. Copyright 1971 by Guideposts Associates, Inc., Carmel, New York 10512

for a minute before it connected unexpectedly with the
memory of my first bowling lesson, given me by my father.
Strange that something as unprofound as a bowling technique could rescue me from the quicksand of unproduc-
tivity, but as soon as I started applying a bowling formula
to my life goals, things began to happen. I earned my
master's degree, gained a pilot's license and launched a
career in writing, in addition to reaching some other less
ambitious goals. But more important, it helped me ex-
change my vague feeling of unworthiness for the bold
hope that maybe my life could really count for something
after all.

I'd like to share the ways in which the "aim yourself"
technique has worked for me, in the hope that it might
help you, too.

The first step in my father's bowling formula is: Pick a
spot just in front of you that's in line with the center pin.
When I applied that advice to my life, I realized I had to
aim toward one goal at a time and that each goal had to be
exact. My vague desire to be a better housekeeper was not
good enough. I had to really pin it down and resolve to
"clean out the linen closet and the coat closet today."

I also learned to choose goals that I could start on right
now and accomplish within a limited time. I had always
thought that someday I'd like to go back to college and get
a master's degree, but the prospect was so overwhelming
that I kept putting it off. So instead of aiming for my
degree, I signed up for just one class. Aiming for a spot
"just in front of me" made it easier to begin. We need
long-term goals, too, but I have found that we reach
broader, distant goals by the route of today's well-aimed
single steps.

Since the "spot" must be "in line with the center pin," I

try to test each goal with these questions: Will it make me more nearly the kind of person I want to be? Will its accomplishment further my long-term goals? Is it important?

After I have selected a goal that is exact, short-term and in line with my long-term goals, I am ready for step two:

Aim your whole self toward the goal. In bowling, golf, archery or any other sport where aim is important, the whole body has to get into the act. Single-mindedness is just as important in aiming for short-term goals in life. Here are some tricks that have helped keep my attention focused on current goals.

As soon as I have chosen a goal, I do something *right then* toward its accomplishment. When I resolved to paint the bedroom, I ordered the green paint; when I decided to take flying lessons, I made an appointment for my first lesson.

I tell someone about my goal. This makes it harder for me to talk myself out of it later.

I make three copies of the goal, including time limit, placing these reminders by things I use every day—in my silverware drawer, on the refrigerator door, in the coat pocket that holds my keys. Every time I run across one of these reminders during the day, I try to stop what I'm doing and make some further effort toward my goal. If I can't stop, I can at least plan what my next step will be and exactly when I will do it.

As I sit down to each meal or snack during the day, I try to remember to picture my goal as already accomplished and say a short prayer of thanksgiving.

After I have done everything I can toward the accomplishment of a particular goal, I take the third and final step: Let go of the ball. I turn the outcome over to God, knowing that, just as there are physical laws that make a bowling ball keep rolling once it's started, there are also spiritual laws that take over for us after we have chosen an exact goal and aimed our whole self toward it. Sometimes it's hard for me to let go and let God, but I have learned that if I can do just that, the ball I started rolling will continue on its way with the help of God and by His sure laws.

I still give up on goals sometimes. My housekeeping never did improve all that much, and my thumb is not getting any greener; but I find that I'm succeeding far more often than I used to, because the formula keeps my aim short, direct and concentrated. And it's the very best remedy in the world for that I-never-seem-to-get-any-where feeling.**"**

Mrs. Helleberg's wisdom is echoed by the publisher of *Ebony* Magazine, Robert Johnson, who said, "Big goals sometimes appall you. The secret of moving ahead is to set little, more easily reachable goals, all of which finally add up to the big goals."

So in your prayers and thinking set God-directed goals; pray about them to be sure they are right, for if they are not right, they are wrong; and nothing wrong ever turns out right.

Action to get the power:

1. Look for ruts in your life and start getting out of them.

2. Do things that will give you the warm feeling of achievement, even little things.

3. Stop procrastinating. Do what should be done and do it now—now—now!

4. Practice the "Aim yourself" technique.

5. Adopt short-term, little goals. They will add up to big goals.

6. Write your goals on paper and keep them where they are always before you.

7. Pray about your goals to be sure they are right, for only right goals will come right.

VI. *Power to Throw Away Your Personality Crutches*

SOME PEOPLE, being insecure, depend upon crutches to prop up a faltering personality. Faced with a deep inner conflicted feeling of inadequacy and believing they are unable to cope with problems, they go for crutches: drugs, for example, or alcohol or compulsive eating. Or in less dramatic ways they try to compensate for a miserable feeling of inferiority. What such persons really want is the power to change their lives.

One of the specialties of Jesus Christ is the elimination of crutches. Remember the man by the Pool of Bethesda? (John 5:2-15). There was a legend that whenever an angel stirred the water whoever first got in would be healed.

This man had been lying by the pool for years until he had achieved a kind of status among the lame, the halt and the blind.

This position served as a crutch for his mixed-up personality. He made the excuse that he could never get into the water first. The fact was that he did not want to be healed, for then he would have had to face life. But Jesus, who knows the inner working of the human mind, bored straight into his consciousness. "Do you really want to be healed?" He demanded. The man squirmed under His direct gaze but then felt hope for the first time. He answered a firm, "Yes, I do want to be healed." Jesus instructed him to get to his feet, throw away his crutch, primarily a mental one, and really live.

A crutch very widely used today is alcohol. I met a man at a reception who had had several cocktails and definitely showed the effects. "Why do I do this?" he asked. "Actually I don't really like it. But I have a shy streak in me and am tongue-tied in conversation. A few cocktails loosen me up, turning me from an introvert to an extrovert. I am just no good socially without the lift alcohol gives me."

My guess is that there are many who drink for this reason. In effect, they are leaning on a crutch. To be a good conversationalist who really communicates, all you have to do is be up on things. You don't need to hobble around on an alcohol crutch.

The pity is that this kind of dependence can and often does turn into alcoholism, one of the most acute forms of defeat. The alcoholic is truly a crippled personality.

Such a person can be cured, however. One of the most important agencies in this process is Alcoholics Anonymous, whose record of giving people the power to change their lives is phenomenal. We have seen many astonishing recoveries through the power of God. This power is always available, but the alcoholic must come to the point where he depends upon God absolutely, having no reserve dependence upon himself.

Here is an example. A man who had hit bottom was now ready to admit that he had no strength within himself to meet his drinking problem. He went to a hospital for alcoholics where he was given the full treatment. The doctor, a famous man in this field, gave him wise advice, saying, "We have done all for you that we can. However, we do not have the skill to extricate from your mind the reservation that may still be there, and this reservation may lead you back to drinking."

The man then said desperately, "Doctor, if you cannot cure me, who can?"

The doctor smiled. "There is another Physician who has the skill to remove that reservation from your mind. And," he added, "He keeps office in the New Testament. Go to Him and you will be healed."

It was late at night when the alcoholic, walking the streets, came to Marble Collegiate Church, Fifth Avenue at 29th Street in New York City. The church was closed. Then he did a strange thing. He wrote on his business card, "Dear Dr. Jesus: Take me completely. I give myself to You. Please heal me." He shoved the card into the mail slot in the church door. He reports that there passed through his body, from the top of his head to his feet, a sense of warmth, and with it the realization that healing had come.

Like the man by the Pool of Bethesda, the alcoholic was able to throw away his crutch.

Alcohol is only one crutch. There are others. A woman consulted me about being overweight. Her doctor had advised her that she was a "compulsive eater" due to some deep unhappiness. Until that unhappiness was corrected she could eat herself into the grave, he told her. It came out what the unhappiness was. Her husband was going with another woman. I pointed out to her that if she slimmed down and recovered her natural good looks and charm, she could get him back. I explained the compulsive neurosis of eating to compensate for trouble. "But I haven't the moral strength to diet," she complained.

"Then ask God to give you that strength," I said.

She was taught to hold (1) an image of herself as slender and beautiful; (2) an image of restoration with her husband, and (3) an image of God helping her to achieve her goals. She succeeded. She threw away her eating crutch. The erring husband gladly returned.

The point is that, whatever your problem may be, whatever form of crutch may be propping up your personality, you can experience a similar healing and release.

So, in the name of Jesus, throw away your crutch and get the power to change your life.

1. Study yourself and honestly face any crutch upon which you depend. Know yourself, your strengths and weaknesses.

2. Keep this deep personal study going until you see clearly what you must do with yourself.

3. Tell the Lord you want to be changed.

4. Stop using your crutch now.

5. Trust God to help you. He always helps the person who wants to get free from a crutch.

VII. *Power to Enjoy Healthy Living*

"You are the picture of health," I commented to an active businessman. "What is your secret?"

Smilingly he replied, "I aim to be healthy, so I think no sick or disability thoughts. I think health and well-being. God wants us to be healthy, so I cooperate with Him and I feel fine."

I happened to know this man's history and recalled the important part played in his case by good doctors. He came by his present healthy condition the hard way. But it was evident that he considered healthy thinking an important factor in his experience.

It is of course true that you can think yourself sick. You can think yourself weak and ineffective and old. When James A. Farley, former Postmaster General of the United States, was eighty and a robust, healthy man, I asked him how he remained so well with no telltale signs of age.

"Oh," he replied, "I never think any old thoughts."

And just what are old thoughts? Haven't you often heard them expressed, "I just don't feel good," "I'm not what I once was," "Age is catching up with me," "The old days were best," and on and on ad infinitum. . . . all negative thoughts about lessening vigor and depletion of well-being. Such thoughts in themselves have an aging effect, for ultimately we become what we think.

But the effect of vibrant and vital thinking upon health is enormous, for such a thought pattern stimulates God's re-creative force operating within us. God created us in the first place, but He did not stop with that. He also constantly re-creates. We are told that "In him we live, and move, and have our being" (Acts 17:28). This reminds us that if we keep in close contact with the Creator in our thoughts, His renewing vitality and energy will constantly tone up our being.

A woman who had been sickly for years became a well person having amazing energy. I had not seen her for several years and was amazed at the changed condition of health which was so evident. Asked how she had accomplished such a reversal, she put her finger to her mouth and then to her head, "It all depends upon what you eat and what you think."

What we take into the body can either nourish or poison it. What we take into mind can either strengthen body and spirit or it can cause them to become unhealthy. Indeed, nothing is quite so destructive to the whole being and personality as an unhealthy thought pattern.

Dr. Smiley Blanton, the famous psychiatrist, always declared that "anxiety is the great modern plague." That is what was resulting in ill health for thousands, this great doctor believed.

Still another doctor once told me of a man who actually died of "grudgitis," a long-held hate. Another of his patients, cured of hate, experienced a remarkable rejuvenation of physical well-being. "The only thing wrong with him," said the doctor, "was that his evil thoughts had made his entire physical body react sluggishly; hence, the feelings of ill health." New thinking brought about by forgiveness and love revitalized this patient.

Once, after a sermon, a woman came forward who complained of constant itching, especially in church. She bared her arm to show me a rash which to me was not apparent. "Why do I always itch?" she asked piteously.

Becoming interested in the case, I talked with her and soon became aware of a virulent hatred of her sister. She had the obsession that her sister had cheated her out of part of their father's estate.

I talked with her doctor, who said, surprisingly, "She has mental eczema. She itches not in her body, but in her mind; and it's that old hate that is causing it. Cure her of that, and she should be a well person."

After pointing out to this unhappy woman the mental-spiritual mechanism that was causing her physical trouble, we were able to bring her to forgiveness of her sister. A new and friendly relationship was effected, as a result of which in due time the itching sensation ceased.

Some have found vigorous new health through the use

of affirmation, the statement of a desired good spoken in faith. An example is the man who was given the impression that little could be done for him medically. This diagnosis he refused to accept and he looked widely for help. The technique of affirmation was suggested. Accordingly, he daily practiced affirming, "I am a child of God. His health is within me. All the healing forces of God are mine. I will to be well. I will be well." He lived to age 94, a happy, vigorous man. His doctor, who was very proud of him, commented that, whereas he had an unconscious sick psychology, the shift through affirmation to a well psychology stimulated the natural health forces always at work in us.

Another man who enjoys vigorous health goes through a series of physical exercises every morning. Standing tall and breathing deeply, he blesses every organ in his body, thanking God for "making me right and keeping me right."

Take these action steps for the power to change your life and enjoy healthy living:

1. Never think any sick or old thoughts. Think health—think vitality.

2. Repel anxiety. Practice trust in God.

3. Eliminate the disease of hate, resentment, ill will.

4. Practice daily affirmations, giving thanks that God's health is within you now.

5. Conceive of the healing forces of God as operating in your body, mind, spirit.

6. Bless every organ in your body put there by God and cooperate by keeping them functioning well.

A Final Word of Encouragement

PERSONAL change seldom comes easily. What we now are is a result of attitudes and actions over the years. Such patterns resist change. They are habits not easily reversed or eliminated. So do not become discouraged when, having read this part, "The Power to Change Your Life," you find a change in your life is not readily apparent.

For this reason I have stressed the necessity for practice and suggested steps to help you. I can promise that if you consistently and sincerely practice, you will begin to get results, and very soon.

But . . . you cannot change yourself all by yourself. You may stimulate improvement; indeed, by thinking and being willing to change, you may start becoming a better person. However, one basic thing must be added. You must turn your life over to God, who can make you much more than a better person. He makes you a *new* person: "Old things are passed away; . . . all things are become new" (2 Corinthians 5:17). You are a "new creature."

Never be discouraged. If you want a new life you can have it. And the way is through desire, belief, commitment and practice. Old habit tracks in your nature may be worn deep. There will be resistance to change.

But if you have the will to change and if you give it all you've got, trusting in the Lord to supply strength, you will become a changed person. So re-read this part and practice faithfully the teachings outlined. Above all, humbly commit your life to Christ, asking Him to create in you a new mind and heart, and you will gain the power to change your life. God bless you all the way.

PART SIX:

Faith Builders

The Plan of This Part

To BEGIN with, you and I have a definite objective, and it is to help you build a strong, workable faith.

People say, "I know I should have faith, and I want faith. But how do I get it? That is my problem."

In the following pages you will find some answers to that all-important question, answers that have been used by many persons with great results.

I suggest that you first read through this entire part and its faith-building Bible passages to saturate your mind at once with the knowledge that you *can* build your faith. The plan is not at all complicated. You will find that thirteen ways to develop faith are suggested. Why thirteen? Well, for one reason, we believe that a successful method in faith building is to work on one idea for one week. In that period of time you will have mastered it. And thirteen weeks is one-fourth of a year, so that in three months you should have made large strides toward a robust faith.

Benjamin Franklin in his early career was a small printer in Philadelphia and was heavily in debt. He believed he could master the principle of successful living if only he could find a method. And he did find one which made him an American immortal. He set down thirteen principles and determined to master them. He worked on one with all of his might and main for one week and then went on to the next one. When one group was completed he started another. In this way he was able to work through many principles in one year. Late in life Franklin said that to this method more than to anything else in his whole life he owed his success and happiness.

He said, "I hope, therefore, that some of my descendants may follow my example and reap the benefit." We are not going to utilize Franklin's principles, only his method.

As you study this part, note that in connection with each subject we list several Scripture texts. We call them "Faith Builders." There is wonderful power in these Bible passages when they are taken into consciousness and given time to work in your inner life.

So we suggest that each week you memorize the suggested passages; meditate on them, think them over, say them again and again and make them a definite part of your thought life.

Do this sincerely and they will recondition your spiritual life. They will help to change you and in so doing change everything for you.

May we reiterate that "Faith Builders" is a practical spiritual action manual. It can help you if you will work with it as suggested.

God bless you in building a stronger faith.

I. *Start Where You Are*

Perhaps you feel that you have very little faith. But that is no deterrent.

Everything great begins small: trees, people, ideas. So start where you are with whatever faith you do have. That is the first technique in faith building. And the second is this: make sure that little faith is real. As a Faith Builder points out, through faith as small as a mustard seed, and of course that is very small, you can move mountains: that is to say, you can push aside great, mountainous difficulties. The power of the little thing that is vital and full of sincerity cannot be minimized.

Then ask this first question of yourself. How absolutely honest is this little faith that I do have? Next, start whittling away all the irrelevancies and get down to the central essence of faith. Do you believe in God, do you believe in Christ, do you believe that God and Christ are with you and that They will help you? Do you believe in yourself and in life? Belief in a few basic realities is the important factor in building faith.

Finally, don't worry about the mass of things that you feel you are supposed to believe. Simply believe that Jesus Christ is with you, helping you now, and that through Him your life can be changed.

Start where you are. And once again, do not minimize that little faith; just be sure that it is real.

Now take a piece of paper and make a list of the great things that you do believe in. Then let's go to work with that. Read over the list every day for the next week; add to it. Ask God to help your faith to grow.

Commit to memory the Faith Builders listed here and repeat them aloud every morning as you get up and every evening as you go to bed.

You have now made the all-important beginning.

FAITH BUILDERS

And Jesus said unto them . . . verily I say unto you, If ye have faith as a grain of mustard seed, ye shall say unto this mountain, Remove hence to yonder place; and it shall remove: and nothing shall be impossible unto you. (Matthew 17:20)

Verily I say unto you, Whosoever shall not receive the kingdom of God as a little child shall in no wise enter therein. (Luke 18:17)

Behold, I have set before thee an open door, and no man can shut it: for thou hast a little strength, and hast kept my word, and hast not denied my name. (Revelation 3:8)

SUGGESTION: Read and study John, Chapter one. It has something to say about beginnings.

II. *Really Want to Have Faith*

THERE IS considerable difference between saying what you want and actually deeply wanting it.

If with all your heart you really *want* faith you can have it. But if you only say you want faith nothing much will happen.

There is the realizable desire. When a desire is soul deep, when it is longing in depth, all of the inner forces of your nature conspire to bring about a realization of the desire. But when what you want is superficial, it remains as a frustration, for there is no gathering of inner power to achieve it.

"If with all your heart"—that is the principle of attainment. If with all of yourself you want a strong faith, one which can move mountains and overcome the impossibilities and stand up to all difficulties and lead you into the basic joys of this life, you can have it.

So, before proceeding further ask yourself how far you are willing to go down the sometimes hard road to this faith. Will you exercise the discipline and the effort required? Have you got what it takes to keep on going when the going becomes hard? Can you avoid letting discouragement defeat you?

And the answer, of course, is that you can do all these things if with all your heart you want and mean to develop a strong, workable and joyous faith.

If you are not sure that you really want faith, ask God to make you want it. He is the God of the great desires. He plants them in us and develops them.

Every day declare and affirm, "I want faith, I want it with all my heart. I believe faith is being developed in me now."

Again I suggest you memorize the following Faith Builders and repeat them to yourself every morning and evening, and often during the day.

Pray for faith, think faith, exercise faith, read about faith, affirm faith.

FAITH BUILDERS

For as he thinketh in his heart, so is he.

(Proverbs 23:7)

For where your treasure is, there will your heart be also.   (Matthew 6:21)

But as many as received him, to them gave he power to become the sons of God, even to them that believe on his name.   (John 1:12)

Call unto me, and I will answer thee, and show thee great and mighty things, which thou knowest not.

(Jeremiah 33:3)

SUGGESTION: Matthew, Chapter five, may be helpful.

III. *Faith Is a Fight, a Struggle*

An old hymn says, "Fight the good fight with all thy might." And what is that good fight but the battle with yourself to believe; it is the struggle against pervasive doubt.

The late Dr. Smiley Blanton, great psychiatrist, great human being, deep Christian, used to say that he could help any person to become well if he could get that person to put up a real fight within himself to believe.

His point was, of course, that people develop fear and anxiety and all manner of emotional troubles because they do not have deep inner security, the kind that faith produces.

Therefore, as he reiterated again and again, the first element in healing is to develop the capacity to believe. And this requires struggle, because it runs contrary to those harbored negativisms which give rise to fear.

As one starts to build faith his old doubts will do everything in their power to discourage him. Just when he thinks he has learned to believe, doubt will whisper, "Oh, no, you don't." When he believes that he is going to gain the victory of faith, doubt will sneer, "Oh, no, you haven't."

Doubt will try to confuse him and make him think that faith is an illusion.

What, then, can you do? The answer is simple and direct: Stand up to your doubt; vigorously dispute with your doubt; take authority over your doubt. One man personalizes doubts and talks out loud to them. He lectures them, "You sit down and keep still." And again, "Go away, I don't believe in you, untrustworthy doubts. I won't listen to you any more." He found this practice very rewarding.

Try some such method. View yourself as the absolute master of your doubts. And be ever on the alert, for doubts will sneak up on you when your guard is down.

Remember always that faith is a fight against disbelief, a struggle against doubt!

FAITH BUILDERS

Fight the good fight of faith, lay hold on eternal life. (I Timothy 6:12)

But let us, who are of the day, be sober, putting on the breastplate of faith and love; and for a helmet, the hope of salvation. (I Thessalonians 5:8)

For whatsoever is born of God overcometh the world: and this is the victory that overcometh the world, even our faith. (I John 5:4)

I have fought a good fight, I have finished my course, I have kept the faith. (II Timothy 4:7)

SUGGESTION: Colossians, Chapter three, can be helpful.

IV. *Keep Jesus in Mind*

As you struggle and fight against doubts in attempting to grow a strong faith, great help will come if you keep Jesus always in mind.

He understands you fully. He is aware that in all men good and evil are always at war. He even knows how, when we want the good, we are still attracted by the bad.

He is perfectly aware of the struggle incessantly taking place in that unseen battlefield, the human mind.

The great first thing to keep saying to yourself is, "Jesus loves me." Remember that old hymn of childhood, "Jesus loves me, this I know. For the Bible tells me so." That old song tells the truth.

When the struggle gets hard and doubt and indecision gang up on you and the thought comes that maybe you cannot ever become the kind of person you want to be, with the quality of faith you desire to have, remember and affirm that Jesus will see you through for He loves you.

Many years ago a great Christian scholar by the name of Henry Drummond suggested that if you think of Jesus even for two minutes every day the whole day will be different. So sit down, close your eyes and for two minutes think of nothing else, only Jesus.

The poet William Wordsworth used the method of saying over a passage from the words of Jesus. Then he would reflectively ask himself, "I wonder what was the tone of voice when He said that? What was the look on His face when He uttered those words?" This practice made Jesus very real to him.

Therefore, do not keep your mind on your weaknesses and your doubts but keep Jesus in mind. Try to hear His voice spiritually and touch His hand, keep following after Him and unshakable faith will come.

FAITH BUILDERS

Jesus saith unto him, I am the way, the truth, and the life: no man cometh unto the Father, but by me.
(John 14:6)

For God so loved the world, that he gave his only begotten Son, that whosoever believeth in him should not perish, but have everlasting life.
(John 3:16)

But the Lord is faithful, who shall stablish you, and keep you from evil.
(II Thessalonians 3:3)

Wherefore, seeing we also are compassed about with so great a cloud of witnesses, let us lay aside every weight, and the sin which doth so easily beset us, and let us run with patience the race that is set before us, Looking unto Jesus the author and finisher of our faith; who for the joy that was set before him endured the cross, despising the shame, and is set down at the right hand of the throne of God.
(Hebrews 12:1, 2)

SUGGESTION: Matthew, Chapter nine, is one of many chapters telling how Jesus helped people.

v. *Live the Life of Prayer*

It is not possible to develop a strong faith without learning to pray.

But you may say: "I really do not know how to pray." Then you must learn. And that is not as difficult as it may seem. We learn by doing, by praying. The first thing to do is just to pray and pray regularly.

How much time each day are you now devoting to prayer—five minutes, two minutes or none at all? Let's be honest about it. How can you meet the problems of life with faith if you are giving such a meager amount of time to prayer? Your daily program should make a place for a few minutes of prayer and meditation every morning and every night. Have a regular time to pray.

But there is another method which some have found effective. It is, in effect, carrying out the Biblical advice to pray without ceasing. Dr. Frank Laubach used what he called flash or fragmentary prayers. If he was about to make a telephone call, he offered a quick prayer asking for guidance in the conversation. In signing a letter, he offered a short prayer for the person to whom it was addressed. When you read a tragic story in the newspaper, say a brief prayer for the persons involved.

Another method involves "shooting" prayers at people. For example, you pass a man on the street who looks discouraged and despondent. "Shoot" a prayer at him as you pass. Dr. Laubach said he had known people to turn in surprise and look at him, indicating that the prayer reached them.

As problems occur or decisions arise, turn for a flashing second or two to God, asking advice and guidance.

This practice causes exciting things to happen. But beyond that it definitely gets you into the habitual psychology of prayer. Few procedures will so quickly and effectively build faith. Soon you will become a walking, living personification of prayer and faith.

FAITH BUILDERS

Pray without ceasing.   (I Thessalonians 5:17)

Evening, and morning, and at noon, will I pray, and cry aloud: and he shall hear my voice.   (Psalm 55:17)

Therefore I say unto you, What things soever ye desire, when ye pray, believe that ye receive them, and ye shall have them.   (Mark 11:24)

And he spake a parable unto them to this end, that men ought always to pray, and not to faint.

(Luke 18:1)

Confess your faults one to another, and pray one for another, that ye may be healed. The effectual fervent prayer of a righteous man availeth much. (James 5:16)

SUGGESTION: The 11th Chapter of Mark will be helpful.

VI. *Know that God Loves You*

WE ARE TOLD that God is love; that He takes note of every sparrow that falls and even the hairs of our head are numbered. This means that the least among us is very important to God.

God is described as a forgiving, loving Father. In building faith it is of first importance to integrate this truth into your mind. Every day say aloud, "I am a child of God. God is interested in the smallest detail of my life. God loves me."

If any doubt arises, reaffirm and reiterate God's love and hold to that thought until you know it for a fact.

A thoughtful man asked, "What is the greatest truth in the world?" I turned the question back to him and he said, "It is that we are not alone."

In building your faith emphasize the great truth that no matter how dark it gets, how lonely you feel, or how you may experience rejection, you are not alone. Repeat that every night as you go to sleep and whenever difficulty comes. "I am not alone. God is with me."

Because God loves you and is always with you, you can have confidence that if you live His way to the best of your ability and put your trust in Him, you will develop a faith that will withstand every shock in this life.

A method for meeting difficult responsibilities that can be of immeasurable help is simply to say: "God, please stay with me and help me and I will try to do the best I can." And then add confidently the affirmation: "Thank you, God, for helping me *now*."

FAITH BUILDERS

We love him, because he first loved us.　(I John 4:19)

The Lord is good to all: and his tender mercies are over all his works.　(Psalm 145:9)

The Lord hath appeared of old unto me, saying, Yea, I have loved thee with an everlasting love: therefore with lovingkindness have I drawn thee.

(Jeremiah 31:3)

Why art thou cast down, O my soul? and why art thou disquieted in me? hope thou in God: for I shall yet praise him for the help of his countenance.

(Psalm 42:5)

He that loveth not, knoweth not God; for God is love.　(I John 4:8)

That Christ may dwell in your hearts by faith; that ye, being rooted and grounded in love, May be able to comprehend with all saints what is the breadth, and length, and depth, and height; And to know the love of Christ, which passeth knowledge, that ye might be filled with all the fulness of God.

(Ephesians 3:17-19)

SUGGESTION: Read Psalm 91 which describes how God loves you.

VII. *Remember God Watches Over You*

W HATEVER your circumstances you can be sure that God watches over you. Because He loves you, and since God Himself is love, you can be confident that you are never out of His sight, nor His loving concern.

How can you make yourself believe this? First, reiterate it to yourself. Reiteration is a powerful method of persuading the mind to accept a truth. Epictetus called it the most classical of all studies. It brings about acceptance.

Thank God constantly for watching over you and protecting you. After every journey thank Him for His protecting care. In every difficult situation thank Him for seeing you through.

Sit down occasionally and on paper make a list of the times in your life you have experienced God's providential care. That list will be so impressive that it will deepen your faith.

Visualize your loved ones as always being protected by the everlasting arms and supported by the great hand of God. In such manner you will be sending out protecting and guiding thoughts which God will use for their protection. Help God to protect your loved ones and yourself.

A final technique is to commit to memory many of the passages which deal with the protective love of God. Every day say some of them to yourself, meditating upon them with gratitude. Use the Faith Builders on this page and others that you may discover for yourself.

FAITH BUILDERS

The Lord is nigh unto all them that call upon him, to all that call upon him in truth. (Psalm 145:18)

Trust in the Lord with all thine heart; and lean not unto thine own understanding. In all thy ways acknowledge him, and he shall direct thy paths. (Proverbs 3:5, 6)

In God have I put my trust: I will not be afraid what man can do unto me. (Psalm 56:11)

Humble yourselves therefore under the mighty hand of God, that he may exalt you in due time: Casting all your care upon him; for he careth for you. (I Peter 5:6, 7)

Cast thy burden upon the Lord, and he shall sustain thee: he shall never suffer the righteous to be moved. (Psalm 55:22)

If I take the wings of the morning, and dwell in the uttermost parts of the sea; Even there shall thy hand lead me, and thy right hand shall hold me. (Psalm 139:9, 10)

SUGGESTION: Read John, Chapter 14, which further tells of the loving care of God.

VIII. *Stand Up to Your Fears with Faith*

THE SECOND greatest force in the world is fear. And it has incredible power to destroy people. It is impossible to estimate the number of lives it has ruined.

But let us not dwell on the second greatest force in the world but rather on the *greatest* force of all, and that is faith. Fear is very strong, but faith is much stronger. Faith can actually cancel out fear.

The first step in building faith against fear is to stand up to your fears with faith. And so incredibly strong is faith that even a little faith, if it's real, can undercut enormous fear.

Another technique in the faith building process is to discover why you have fears. Counseling may be required to gain this insight.

The third step is something not to do. Do not go skulking through life, being timorous and afraid. Say to yourself, and mean it: "In the name of God and by the power of Jesus Christ I hereby stand up to my fears with faith. I am no longer afraid."

If you do not weaken, your fears one by one will finally slink away. But you must be vigilant. If you let down your faith, your fears will try to return. You have given hospitality to them for so long that they feel at home in your mind. Sadly, you may even miss them. But deliberately become obstinate, gloriously obstinate. Tell yourself that with God's help you will not let them come back. Keep filling your mind so full of faith that there will no longer be any room for fears.

FAITH BUILDERS

The Lord is my light and my salvation: whom shall I fear? the Lord is the strength of my life; of whom shall I be afraid? When the wicked, even mine enemies and my foes, came upon me to eat up my flesh, they stumbled and fell.
Though a host should encamp against me, my heart shall not fear: though war should rise against me, in this will I be confident.   (Psalm 27:1-3)

For I the Lord thy God will hold thy right hand, saying unto thee, Fear not; I will help thee.
                                                                    (Isaiah 41:13)

Watch ye, stand fast in the faith, quit you like men, be strong.   (I Corinthians 16:13)

Yea, though I walk through the valley of the shadow of death, I will fear no evil: for thou art with me; thy rod and thy staff they comfort me.   (Psalm 23:4)

There is no fear in love; but perfect love casteth out fear.   (I John 4:18)

SUGGESTION: Read the 11th Chapter of Hebrews, often called "the Westminster Abbey of the Scriptures."

IX. *Add Up Your Securities*

ONE REASON people have weak or little faith is due to a continual emphasis on their insecurity. As a result, they develop a haunting feeling that something bad is going to happen. Over them constantly rests a cloud of sinister uncertainty.

One cannot mentally dwell upon insecurity without feeling insecure. And faith has great difficulty in taking root in a soil of insecurity.

To counteract this unhappy situation and unpropitious influence in your life begin at once to dwell upon and emphasize the security factors in your life. Add up your "securities."

If you felt poor but had a number of securities in the safety deposit box in the bank you could go there, add them up and depart feeling pretty secure financially.

In similar manner make a list of the dependable and secure factors with which you are surrounded, such as: the good earth, whose seed time and harvest can be depended upon. The sun never fails to come back and shine through the clouds. You have the love of your wife or husband, the love of children. Your heart still beats. You can eat and walk and think.

Go on and add to the list and over it all write the words "God" and "Jesus Christ." As you habitually add up your securities, feelings of insecurity will diminish. Your faith will grow stronger.

FAITH BUILDERS

The Lord is my rock, and my fortress, and my deliverer; my God, my strength, in whom I will trust; my buckler, and the horn of my salvation, and my high tower.   (Psalm 18:2)

I can do all things through Christ which strengtheneth me.   (Philippians 4:13)

Fear thou not; for I am with thee: be not dismayed; for I am thy God: I will strengthen thee; yea, I will help thee; yea, I will uphold thee with the right hand of my righteousness.   (Isaiah 41:10)

Therefore will not we fear, though the earth be removed, and though the mountains be carried into the midst of the sea.   (Psalm 46:2)

And we know that all things work together for good to them that love God, to them who are the called according to his purpose.   (Romans 8:28)

SUGGESTION: Read the 90th Psalm.

x. *Practice Your Faith*

IN THE development of any skill, continual practice is required. To become proficient in music or on the golf course or in anything, practice makes one, if not perfect, at least more competent.

So, in developing faith, practice faith in every possible situation. To do this is to use positive expressions such as: "This project is going to turn out well; this problem will come out satisfactorily." Never say: "This project is doomed to failure; this problem is too difficult." Be affirmative in your attitudes.

What we say about a situation determines how we think about it and finally what we do about it. Attitude largely determines activity; so watch your attitude and make it one of faith. By practicing positive attitudes, your faith will grow stronger and results will be creative.

In practicing faith, read inspirational material—books and articles by people who believe and about individuals who have achieved through faith. Of course, the greatest book is the Bible, but inspirational books will also help. Saturate your mind with them.

Associate with inspirational people, with persons who have themselves developed faith. Such associations will definitely strengthen your own faith. Someone else who has struggled through to a creative faith will inspire and motivate you.

For this reason, become active in the church. Unhappily, there are negative people in the church; but the proportion of faith-minded people is higher there.

FAITH BUILDERS

The Lord hath done great things for us; whereof we are glad.   (Psalm 126:3)

He layeth up sound wisdom for the righteous: he is a buckler to them that walk uprightly.   (Proverbs 2:7)

Behold, now is the accepted time; behold, now is the day of salvation.   (II Corinthians 6:2)

A new heart also will I give you, and a new spirit will I put within you.   (Ezekiel 36:26)

SUGGESTION: Read Matthew, Chapter 7. It will be helpful to commit verses 24-27 to memory.

XI. *Learn to Trust*

LEARNING to trust is important in building faith.

Actually, we live on a trust basis every day. We trust the motorman of a train, the driver of a bus, the pilot of an airplane. We put our lives completely into the hands of those men. And we are quite willing to do so, for we have faith in them. And usually we don't even know them.

Here we are on this earth, a whirling island in the sky. Our lives are in the hands of Someone who directs its orbits and laws. Whether we like it or not, we are wholly dependent upon God, so we must trust Him. In a practical sense from this viewpoint we *do* trust Him without giving it a thought.

But how may we trust God in life's daily affairs? One way is to know and love God. We trust human beings whom we know and love. And when you know God, His goodness, kindness and faithfulness, you will trust Him, for you will love Him. He will fulfill your trust. He will never let you down.

Do the best you can about everything and trust the outcome to God. Confidently trust Him to handle things beyond your efforts. He knows the facts. Every day, especially when you feel uncertain, try saying the following to yourself:

1. I put my life in God's hands.
2. I will trust God's guidance.
3. I leave the outcome to God.

Live close to God until you begin to think His thoughts after Him. Believe that He has the answers to your perplexities. The closer you live to Him the more sensitively will you pick up His thoughts for you. This will induce a profound confidence. This will build up your faith.

FAITH BUILDERS

The Lord is good, a stronghold in the day of trouble; and he knoweth them that trust in him.   (Nahum 1:7)

Behold, God is my salvation; I will trust, and not be afraid: for the Lord Jehovah is my strength and my song; he also is become my salvation.   (Isaiah 12:2)

The God of my rock; in him will I trust: he is my shield, and the horn of my salvation, my high tower, and my refuge, my saviour; thou savest me from violence.   (II Samuel 22:3)

For thou art my hope, O Lord God: thou art my trust from my youth.   (Psalm 71:5)

Though he slay me, yet will I trust in him: (Job 13:15)

SUGGESTION: Read Isaiah, Chapter 55. It tells what trust can mean to you.

XII. *Know the God of the Impossible*

THE PERSON who believes that seemingly impossible things can happen will develop an incredibly strong faith. In fact, you can measure your faith by your concept of the impossible.

People who grow a great faith are those who believe that nothing is too good to be true. Little minds see only little things and as a result only little things ever happen. But big minds see big things happening, for big faith brings big results.

An upstate New York farmer told me once: "Think big, pray big, believe big, see God as big, and life will be big."

Never build a case against yourself. Never settle for that which is small. Only be willing to accept from life the big things that life has to give to those who have a large faith in a God of greatness.

Practice letting your mind stretch itself. Deliberately think bigger and bigger thoughts of faith. Conceive of greater things occurring through your faith. Take a deep breath and venture out beyond your depth. Do not hug the shore; do not fear high places. You can go as far as you think you can. Think high and wide and deep and far.

You will never go any higher than your thoughts or your prayers or your faith. So practice stretching your faith. You can never stretch it higher than God. But you can stretch it to Him.

FAITH BUILDERS

And this is the confidence that we have in him, that, if we ask any thing according to his will, he heareth us. (I John 5:14)

And he said, The things which are impossible with men are possible with God. (Luke 18:27)

But Jesus ... said unto them, With men this is impossible; but with God all things are possible. (Matthew 19:26)

Jesus said unto him, If thou canst believe, all things are possible to him that believeth. (Mark 9:23)

Cast not away therefore your confidence, which hath great recompense of reward. (Hebrews 10:35)

SUGGESTION: Read Luke, Chapter 8, which tells of some of the great things Jesus does.

XIII. *Commit Yourself*

W E HAVE saved until the last the greatest Faith Builder
of all, which is to commit yourself to God and to Christ.

What do we mean by *commit yourself?* It is to give
yourself to the Lord. Another way of saying it is to
surrender your life to His control, to follow His guidance
in all that you do and are.

I would like to tell you about a man who learned the
greatest spiritual truth of all. He was under much stress
from pressure and trouble. He came to the point where he
surrendered his life to Christ. He simply said, "Lord, I give
myself to You." His faith prior to that time was weak and
inadequate and he was lacking in joy and creative power.

But after he made the surrender and fully gave himself
to Christ he found his faith growing ever stronger. New joy
came to him and he was able to work more effectively than
at any other time in his life.

Another man who achieved great faith from small and
weak beginnings had on his desk a framed statement:
"What would Jesus do?" This constant challenge so
changed his life from weakness to power that he had the
statement made up for others. He gave over three thousand of them to people everywhere, many of whom found
strong faith and new life.

I cite these personal stories, and could tell of many
others, that I might say in conclusion that what is written
here is not theoretical but the result of personal spiritual
experience. These things we have written will work. Many
have personally experienced their workability. So can you.

Many people, too numerous to mention, bear testimony that the way to a strong faith is through the surrendered life. Give yourself to God in faith and He will give Himself to you. The result will be a powerful faith strong enough to move huge mountains which heretofore have seemed impossible barriers. Make your own sincere commitment now.

FAITH BUILDERS

That if thou shalt confess with thy mouth the Lord Jesus, and shalt believe in thine heart that God hath raised him from the dead, thou shalt be saved. For with the heart man believeth unto righteousness; and with the mouth confession is made unto salvation.   (Romans 10:9, 10)

Commit thy way unto the Lord; trust also in him; and he shall bring it to pass.   (Psalm 37:5)

For we are made partakers of Christ, if we hold the beginning of our confidence steadfast unto the end.
(Hebrews 3:14)

SUGGESTION: Read Matthew, Chapter 26, to deepen your commitment.

ACTION TECHNIQUES DESCRIBED
IN *FAITH BUILDERS*

To start, list the things you believe in—God, Christ, Their help for you, etc; study this list daily and add to it as you grow.

Affirm "I want Faith, I want it with all my heart."

Personalize doubt and banish it, speaking out loud to it.

Think only of Jesus for two minutes.

Have a regular time to pray, morning and night.

Use "flash" or fragmentary prayers. Try "shooting" prayers at people.

Ask God to stay with you in difficult situations, and affirm that He is helping you *now*.

Make a list of the times you have experienced God's providential care.

Visualize your mind so full of faith that fear is crowded out.

Write down all your "securities," those dependable and secure factors with which you are surrounded.

Read inspirational books, associate with inspiring persons, become active in the church. *Practice your faith.*

Affirm "I put my life in God's hands. I will trust God's guidance. I leave the outcome to God."

Practice stretching your faith—never build a case against yourself.

Put the question "What would Jesus do?" where you will see it daily. *Commit yourself now to Christ.*

PART SEVEN:

The Pocket Cards

INTRODUCTION

Summing It Up

As a boy I had to listen to a lot of speeches and sermons. I'm sure I didn't always appreciate this at the time, but I found that even the most ordinary speakers said some things worth listening to. And the best speakers of all, to my way of thinking, excelled in two things. They used good illustrations, right out of their own experiences, and they summed up what they were talking about in a few simple points that were easy to remember.

That is the way I want to end this book. Here are a few simple suggestions designed to pin down and apply the basic theme.

The way to have God's help with your problems is the way to overcome tension, the way to have the power of enthusiasm, the way to have a good day, the way to have God's protection, the way to have vital energy, the way to eliminate worry, the way to overcome inferiority feelings—as suggested in these Pocket Cards. Put these suggestions into daily practice and you will have a life filled with joy and enthusiasm.

These seven Pocket Cards were originally printed by the Foundation for Christian Living. Soon after Pocket Card No. 4, "The Way to Have God's Protection," was published, we had an urgent request from the Chief of Chaplains of the United States Army for 300,000 copies. We telephoned him and found that he wanted to send this card to the chaplains in every Army command post around the world, so that every soldier could carry a copy in his uniform pocket. And with the help of the many friends who support the work of the Foundation, we not only printed and shipped all 300,000 cards, but supplied many more to fill requests from other branches of the military.

Copies of any of the Pocket Cards are available on request from the Foundation for Christian Living, Pawling, New York 12564. They are printed on a special card stock in a size (2½ by 3¾ inches) that fits any pocket or purse.

Pocket Card No. 1
THE WAY TO HAVE A GOOD DAY
by Norman Vincent Peale

THINK a Good Day. To make the day good you have to see it in your mind as good. Since we become what we think, it follows that events are governed by creative thoughts. Get in the habit of thinking good days and you'll go a long way toward getting what you think.

THANK a Good Day. Thank God in advance for the good day ahead because there can't be a good day without His granting it. Actually, thanking is an affirmative way of thinking.

PLAN a Good Day. You'll never get anywhere with a day unless you plan it. You've got to know what you propose to do with it and where you want to go in it. So make your plan and outline your procedures; organize time and effort.

MAKE a Good Day. Make it your business to put good into the day. If we put bad thoughts, bad attitudes into the day, the day will take on the bad. So put good into the day.

PRAY a Good Day. Start and finish every day with God. In the morning read a little from the Bible, putting the day into God's hands. Pray that we may help make it good for everybody we contact. At night pray again, giving thanks for all the blessings of the day.

GET GOING . . . the good old American principle. It's no good sitting around very long just talking (or even just thinking). You've got to get going—so get going!

Norman Vincent Peale

Pocket Card No. 2
THE WAY TO OVERCOME TENSION
A One-Week Prescription
by Norman Vincent Peale

Read each day's thought several times to perceive its deeper meaning. *Commit it to memory.* When it is firmly lodged in your conscious mind, conceive of it as sinking steadily into your subconscious, there to do its healing work.

Proceed similarly each day.

MONDAY "Peace I leave with you, my peace I give unto you ... Let not your heart be troubled, neither let it be afraid" (John 14:27). (Where it says *you* or *your,* use your own name.)

TUESDAY "Thou wilt keep him in perfect peace, whose mind is stayed on thee: because he trusteth in thee" (Isaiah 26:3).

WEDNESDAY "My presence shall go with thee, and I will give thee rest" (Exodus 33:14).

THURSDAY "Rest in the Lord, and wait patiently for him: fret not thyself" (Psalm 37:7).

FRIDAY "Come unto me, all ye that labour and are heavy laden, and I will give you rest" (Matthew 11:28).

SATURDAY "Let the peace of God rule in your hearts" (Colossians 3:15).

SUNDAY "He maketh me to lie down in green pastures: he leadeth me beside the still waters. He restoreth my soul" (Psalm 23:2,3).

This procedure has freed thousands of people from tension.

Norman Vincent Peale

Pocket Card No. 3
THE WAY TO HAVE
THE POWER OF ENTHUSIASM
by Norman Vincent Peale

1. WANT ENTHUSIASM—really *want* that priceless quality that puts verve, zest and delight into existence. When you profoundly want enthusiasm it will start coming to you.

2. LEARN THAT ENTHUSIASM IS VITAL to successful living. Emerson said "Nothing great was ever achieved without enthusiasm"; and Voltaire rebuffed the cynic: "I prefer the folly of enthusiasm to the indifference of wisdom."

3. KNOW THAT ENTHUSIASM CAN BE CULTIVATED; start believing that you can be an enthusiastic person and thereby attract rather than repulse life's richest values.

4. BEGIN NOW TO THINK AND ACT WITH ENTHUSIASM. Affirm enthusiasm daily, hourly, for we tend to become what we affirm. Think, talk, act enthusiastically and enthusiasm will result.

5. CULTIVATE THE TRUE CHILD-LIKE HEART. Apply the wisdom of Jesus ... that unless we become as little children, having their sense of wonder, we shall miss the best in life. And Huxley's insight: true genius in living is to carry the spirit of the child into old age.

6. PRACTICE BEING EXCITED. Act thrilled by the world, by beauty, by opportunity, by people. Every morning say aloud with enthusiasm "This is the day that the Lord hath made. I will rejoice and be glad in it."

7. DEVELOP A CLOSE RELA-TIONSHIP WITH JESUS. "In Him was life; and the life was the light of men." Live with Jesus and that same life and light—namely, the power of enthusiasm—will be yours.

Norman Vincent Peale

Pocket Card No. 4

THE WAY TO HAVE
GOD'S PROTECTION

by Norman Vincent Peale

Read and commit to your heart Psalm 91, which promises God's protection.

GOD IS EVER PRESENT. Remember that God is always near. His power is surrounding you and your loved ones and your situation. He is "closer . . . than breathing, and nearer than hands and feet" (Tennyson). Reach for Him and accept His protection.

GOD LOVES YOU. Realize that you are very important to God, that His love is all-encompassing. Though you seem to have great problems, God will give you strength to overcome them and will watch over you as His child. Those very problems will have meaning in your future life which you cannot now comprehend.

GOD WATCHES OVER YOU. Visualize the great kindly face of God watching, guiding, protecting you and your loved ones wherever you or those dear to you may go. Thank God every day for His watchful care and affirm: "He is my refuge and my fortress . . . in him will I trust."

GOD'S SECURITY IN AN INSECURE WORLD. Fix in your mind that with God you are secure and protected. God alone is steadfast and unchanging in a world of pain and insecurity. Never project upon a loved one any anxiety or danger thought, but instead surround him with faith. "His truth shall be thy shield and buckler."

PLACE YOURSELF IN GOD'S HANDS. Confidently place your loved ones and yourself in His strong, capable hands, knowing that in those hands no harm can come, only good. "For he shall give his angels charge over thee, to keep thee in all thy ways."

Norman Vincent Peale

Pocket Card No. 5

THE WAY TO HAVE VITAL ENERGY

A Seven Day Program for Maintaining Vitality
by Norman Vincent Peale

MONDAY: Start by anticipating a great week. The practice of anticipation stimulates zest and the zestful person always has energy going for him.

TUESDAY: Energy sags when your thoughts sag, so on this second day pull your thoughts up to the enthusiasm level and hold them there. How to do this? Simply *act* enthusiastic. Act as if you were already enthusiastic and you will tend to be so.

WEDNESDAY: Today firmly cope with two attitudes which siphon off energy: worry and frustration. To cancel them out, think faith, practice faith, affirm faith. Replace negative with positive thoughts.

THURSDAY: Pray away the "gray sickness"—that half awake, half asleep, half alive, half dead feeling that sometimes comes to destroy our energy and force. Pray and act upon alive-type prayers of excitement, joy and gratitude.

FRIDAY: Remind yourself that as a child of God you are the constant recipient of boundless life, health, energy and vitality. Visualize yourself as continually being re-created in body, mind and spirit.

SATURDAY: Today practice the art of slowing down. Relax and try getting yourself into the even rhythm of God who created you. Let life's basic tempo take over. Drop out worry and tension.

SUNDAY: Go to church. For "they that wait upon the Lord shall renew their strength; they shall mount up with wings as eagles; they shall run, and not be weary; and they shall walk, and not faint."

Norman Vincent Peale

Pocket Card No. 6
THE WAY TO ELIMINATE WORRY
by Norman Vincent Peale

To get on top of worry change worry into thinking. Worry sends the mind round and round in the same groove and you never come to any conclusions. Thinking works its way through the problem to an answer. You make progress when you think, but you get nowhere when you worry.

THINK, really think, about the following creative spiritual principles:

SHIFT your attention deliberately from the thing you are worrying about. The mind can only occupy itself with the object of its attention. Give attention to faith, not worry.

CULTIVATE opposites: courage instead of fear, strength instead of weakness, joy instead of sorrow.

ACT "as if." What you act tends to become fact.

DISSECT your worries. Ruthlessly take them apart. You'll find there is very little substance to them.

GET PERSPECTIVE of time and distance. How little our big worries seem and how unimportant in the years after.

TALK life up. Don't talk trouble. It only activates more of it.

FORGET yourself and you will find yourself. You will grow bigger in the great, exciting world once you get outside your little constrictive self-world.

CANCEL negative thoughts with positive ones. Enough of this and you will become positive in your attitudes.

PRACTICE great affirmations like: "God loves me"; "Life is good."

SAY to yourself every day, "I am a child of God." Nothing can ever defeat the partnership of God and you working together.

Norman Vincent Peale

Pocket Card No. 7
THE WAY TO OVERCOME INFERIORITY FEELINGS
by Norman Vincent Peale

1. Form and stamp indelibly upon your mind a mental picture of yourself as a creation of God, able and competent.

2. Whenever a negative thought concerning your personal ability comes to mind, deliberately voice a positive thought to cancel it out.

3. Never build up obstacles in your imagination; mentally depreciate every so-called obstacle.

4. Image yourself as doing what you must do, and doing it well.

5. Practice relaxation and silence daily for 10 minutes.

6. Empty the mind every night.

7. During that empty-minded period, repeat the following ten times:

*I can do all things in Him who
 strengthens me.*
I am with you always.
If God be for us, who can be against us?
*God is our refuge and strength, a very
 present help in trouble.*
Say each ten times.

8. Then make this affirmation every day:
*From this day onward, through the help of
God, I am becoming more and more conscious of all that is good and creative and
positive. All my thoughts are now becoming strong and cheerful and victorious. I
am gaining daily in self-confidence. I am
becoming conscious daily of my own in-
creasing powers. My life is becoming more
effective, more efficient. I am rising now to
a new plane of creative thinking.*

Norman Vincent Peale

Index

Trust, learning to, 178

Upset, being, 62
Understanding, 115
Unfaithfulness, 44
Unhappiness, dealing with, 121-
    22
Unhealthy mental states, 107
Unhealthy thinking, 53, 122

Value of problems, 68-71
Victorious attitude, 27
Victorious life, 5
Victory
    over death, 23
    over misery, 122
    over temptation, 116-18
Visualizing God's help, 140

Visualizing re-creation, 197
Vitality, 17, 28

Ward, Emory, 47
Whitman, Walt, 27
Weakness, 119
Weight problems, 148-149
Wholeness of self, 17
Wisdom, 41, 43
Word of God, 10
Words of Jesus Christ, 4
Worry, 28, 38, 97-98, 196, 198-
    99
Writing out problems, 81
Wrongdoing, 118
Wrong thinking, 53, 107

Zest, 17, 49, 50, 52